The Scottish
of Frederick Chopin

The Scottish Autumn
of
Frederick Chopin

IWO & PAMELA ZAŁUSKI

JOHN DONALD PUBLISHERS LTD
EDINBURGH

ISBN 0 85976 389 7

British Library Cataloguing in Publication Data
A catalogue record for this book is available from the British Library.

Typeset by The Midlands Book Typesetting Company, Loughborough
Printed in Great Britain by J. W. Arrowsmith Ltd, Bristol

Acknowledgements

The Chopin Society, London
The Fryderyk Chopin Society, Warsaw
The Jagiełło Library, Kraków
The Kórnik Library, Kórnik, Poland
Broadwood Pianos, Milton Keynes
The Leighton Library
Strathclyde Regional Archives
Miss Elaine Brown and Miss Gill Sullivan, Kilbarchan Library
Mr Ken Henshelwood, Paisley Library
The Scottish Tourist Board
The Royal Norwegian Embassy
Dr Martha Novak Clinkscale, University of California
Lady Margaret Torphichen, Calder House
Miss Jane Kellett, Edinburgh
Sir Fitzroy Maclean of Dunconnel Bt, Strachur
Mr Charles Maclean, Strachur
Mrs Valerie McIntyre, White House of Milliken, Renfrewshire
Dr Wiktor Tomaszewski, Edinburgh

London, 1993   Iwo & Pamela Załuski

Translations from Polish and French by Iwo Załuski

Contents

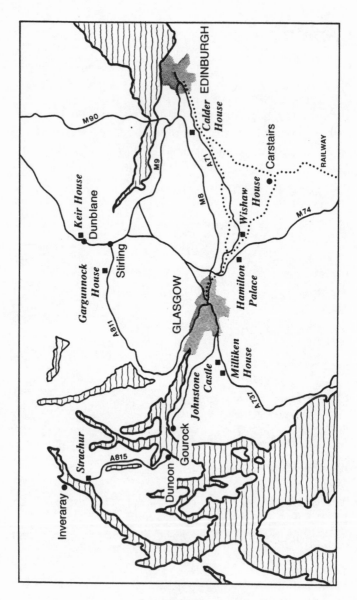

Location map.

CHAPTER ONE

London

Frederick Chopin's first experience on British soil was memorable only inasmuch as he was forced to spend a few miserable hours in Folkestone, recovering from what must have been a rough springtime crossing from Boulogne. It was a nauseating experience for a sick man, for the tuberculosis that was to kill him the following year was by now well established. He had become frail and weak, and was physically a shadow of his former self, although he had never really enjoyed good health. His pianistic style, always delicate and exquisitely mannered, had become so gentle that he no longer played his large-scale works and difficult studies, which exhausted him — as indeed did travel, an occupation generally undertaken in the nineteenth century only by the fit and healthy.

Having recovered sufficiently to continue the ordeal of travelling to London, he ensured that arrangements for the shipment of his favourite piano, a soft-toned Pleyel that had been lent to him by Camille Pleyel himself, were under control, and then he climbed aboard the train and arrived at London Bridge on a bleak Maundy Thursday, 21 April 1848.

There were a number of reasons for Chopin's visit to London. Firstly, he was still smarting from the final break-up, on the steps of Countess Charlotte Marliani's house, of his long-established relationship with the French authoress, George Sand, on 4 March.

Secondly, Paris was in the throes of revolution since the dramatic and clandestine departure of Louis-Philippe, the 'middle-class' King of the French, who had

1

been ousted from power in February of that year; he had sought asylum under the wing of Queen Victoria, who put Claremont, in Esher, at his disposal. The heady days of his tenancy of the throne were now gone, as was the Paris of Liszt, Alkan, Kalkbrenner, Berlioz and Thalberg. Chopin had performed for King Louis-Philippe at the Tuileries on a number of occasions, and although Chopin personally had little time for the King he now missed his patronage and the tone that he had set in his capital over the past decade.

It was the end of an era; elegance, culture and good manners had given way to a new brutalism, which was not to the gentle and immaculately mannered Chopin's liking. Paris, the essential watering hole for wealthy foreign patrons thirsting for art and culture, had lost its identity, and many of its musicians, among them Kalkbrenner, Thalberg and Berlioz, departed from Paris and travelled to England and a warm welcome in London, a city where they could continue to earn money and make a living performing in concerts and recitals and giving lessons to aspiring amateur musicians from the wealthy upper classes. Some of Chopin's former pupils, including Thomas Tellefsen, were also beginning to establish themselves, and were ready to help him with advice and support.

The third, and possibly most significant reason, was Jane Wilhelmina Stirling. She was born at Kippenross House, outside Dunblane, Scotland, on 15 July 1804. Jane was the youngest of thirteen children, the adored and petted daughter of John Stirling, Laird of Kippendavie, and Mary Graham. John Stirling was a prominent member of the well-known middle-class Scottish family who had made a considerable fortune from trade with India. Pictures of 'Jeanie' in her youth show her to have been a very pretty girl, although her nose was considered too long for real beauty.

Her father died in 1816, when she was only twelve; and when her mother died, four years later, Jane was taken in hand by her widowed elder sister Katherine Erskine, who appears to have seen off any potential suitors for Jane, preferring to keep her as a constant companion in her widowhood.

In 1826 the now wealthy and inseparable sisters set off for Paris. In common with many other young ladies of means from Britain, a sojourn in the heady atmosphere of the French capital was *de rigueur*. They soon became fully involved in the Parisian experience, and decided to stay on indefinitely.

In the Autumn of 1840, they first met Chopin, who had recently returned to Paris after his abortive trip to Majorca with George Sand. Within two years Jane had become Chopin's piano pupil, and her admiration for him grew, and with it her devotion and affection. She became a very proficient pianist, and Chopin once told her: 'One day you will play very, very well,' a judgement not lightly bestowed. Her repertoire covered the greater part of Chopin's output, even to the more difficult works, including the Concerto in F minor, the Sonata in B minor and the Fantasia in F minor, all of which require a high degree of technical excellence. But one of her favourites was the less demanding Prelude in C minor Op. 28 No. 20; she referred to this rich, chorale-like Largo as *la Prière*. Chopin was very touched by her generosity of spirit, her kindness and her solicitousness, and in 1842 he dedicated his Nocturne in F Minor Op. 55 No. 1 to her, as well as the Nocturne in E flat Op. 55 No. 2 the following year.

In the spring of 1848, with Louis-Philippe gone and unrest in the air, Paris emptied of foreign patronage, and Jane and Katherine returned to their house in London. Jane begged Chopin to join the exodus, promising him success and fortune in the English capital.

With nothing whatsoever to lose, Chopin let out his Paris apartment, and followed her across the Channel to England.

Jane had arranged an apartment for him at 10 Bentinck Street, just off Cavendish Square, and saw to every fine detail for his convenience, even going as far as to ensure that monogrammed writing paper was available for his use, and that his favourite drinking chocolate was waiting for him.

Chopin, however, was not impressed by the rooms which were too expensive for his resources. He had come to London to make money rather than spend it, and he promptly asked Karol Szulczewski, a fellow Pole, to find him something cheaper. Szulczewski acted as the London agent for the Polish government 'in exile', which was situated at the Hotel Lambert in Paris, under the leadership of Prince Adam Czartoryski. He was also the secretary to the London-based Association of Friends of Poland, of which the President was the Scot, Lord Dudley Stuart, Member of Parliament for Arundel.

Meanwhile Chopin went to Kingston-upon-Thames to visit various friends who had come over from France with Louis-Philippe, and who had congregated within easy reach of the exiled king's Surrey quarters. He stayed with them for the Easter week-end celebrations.

On his return he found that Szulczewski had successfully obtained alternative accommodation for him. The day that he moved into the fine, large rooms at 48 Dover Street, the sun came out for the first time since he had arrived in London. In the apartment he found three pianos, an Erard lent by its maker, the Pleyel that he had brought with him from Paris, and a Broadwood loaned by the man who was to become one of his most useful acquaintances in London.

LONDON

Henry Broadwood constituted the third generation of
the great English piano-making dynasty that had been
started by his Scots-born grandfather, John Broadwood.
His father James had now retired, and Henry had taken
over the family business. He saw in Chopin not only a
useful pianist, but also a true friend. He had taken a
great liking to Chopin and went to the most extraordinary lengths to smooth his path, even to the extent of
providing a softer mattress when Chopin complained
that his bed was hard!

Chopin's many acquaintances in London had rallied
round, and he began to complain that his days were
taken up by the calls he had to pay and the constant stream of visitors. He had already met many
London socialites in Paris, including quite a few of
the ladies that had taken piano lessons from him;
and now they descended on him, taking him under
their wing and introducing him to London society on
its home ground.

Chopin's first real engagement was on 15 May at
Stafford House — today Lancaster House in the Mall,
but then the residence of the Duchess of Sutherland
— at which Queen Victoria and Prince Albert were
present. Although the Queen listened with apparent
interest, Prince Albert actually went closer to the piano
to watch Chopin playing. But there was no follow-up by
way of an invitation to Windsor, and the Queen did not
deem Chopin's performance at the concert worthy of
mention in her diary of that night.

By June he had at least five pupils, including Lady
Christopher and Lady Parke, the daughter of the Duchess of Rutland. They each paid him a guinea per hour's
lesson, which were more social than musical events,
since some of them, in true dilettante style, left after
just a few sessions, able to claim that they had been
taught by Chopin.

He also sold two Waltzes, in D flat and C sharp minor from Op. 64 to Cramer, Beale & Co.

But his living expenses were high, as the rent on his apartment was 10 guineas a week and he needed a carriage to get from house to house. What was more, his health was deteriorating steadily in the polluted London air, and he increasingly needed help and support.

His Italian servant had proved to be lazy and unreliable. He cheated Chopin financially, constantly grumbling and mocking him behind his back, so Chopin sacked him on 1 July and in his place engaged an Irishman called Daniel.

In Chopin's eyes Daniel was the equal of any gentleman. He was urbane and handsome, spoke fluent French and showed considerable tact and diplomacy in dealing with Chopin's changing moods. During the last fifteen months of Chopin's life this loyal and devoted servant remained with him. There is no record of either his surname, or what became of him afterwards.

Chopin was invited to play with the London Philharmonic, but refused, saying that he could not cope with their custom of having only one rehearsal, and that in public. But the real reason was that he knew that he could no longer play with a full orchestra and that in a large concert hall his playing would be drowned. It would also entail playing his concertos and the large-scale early works for piano and orchestra such as the *Krakowiak* and the *Andante Spianato* and *Grande Polonaise Brillante*, which would have been far too strenuous for his enfeebled constitution.

Also, he did not think very much of the London Philharmonic Orchestra, comparing them to roast beef or turtle soup: strong, pungent and nothing more.

Meanwhile, he was much in demand for soirées and matinées, which suited his delicate and quiet style, and where he was able to play what he liked playing best

— the Nocturnes, Waltzes, Mazurkas and the Berceuse. George Hogarth, writing in the *Daily News* — or 'Delinius' as Chopin quaintly and phonetically refers to the periodical — on 10 July described Chopin's style:

> He accomplishes enormous difficulties, but so quietly, so smoothly and with such constant delicacy and refinement that the listener is not sensible of their real magnitude. It is the exquisite delicacy, with the liquid mellowness of his tone, and the pearly roundness of his passages of rapid articulation which are the peculiar features of his execution, while his music is characterised by freedom of thought, varied expression and a kind of romantic melancholy which seems the natural mood of the artist's mind.

For a private matinée recital Chopin received 25 guineas, which was not as much as he could bring in from a public concert with admission by ticket.

The first of these took place at 99 Eaton Place, the Belgravia home of the singer, Mrs Adelaide Sartoris, on the afternoon of 23 June. There is a plaque on the house to commemorate the event.

This concert was followed by another on the afternoon of 7 July at the home of Lord Falmouth, 2 St James's Square, at which Pauline Viardot sang to his mazurkas. This house was destroyed in the Second World War.

Both these concerts were arranged by Henry Broadwood. They netted £300, a welcome sum, because the landlord saw that Chopin was making a lot of money and promptly put up the rent on his apartment to £20 a week.

In the meantime, the London air did not agree with the frail musician; not surprisingly, as it was thick with coal-dust and fog, which did his consumptive lungs no good whatever. He described how on some mornings he thought he was going to cough himself to death. He was spitting blood, and was generally tired, depressed and miserable. He tried his best to deaden his feelings, and made every effort to get out and about so as not to be left to brood alone; but this proved to be a considerable strain, since all the visits, dinners and soirées were definitely taking their toll on his health.

Gregarious though he was, Chopin suffered another great setback in not being able to speak English; he spoke only French and Polish. Despite having been taught English in Warsaw by a drunken Irishman by the name of McCartney, despite all the music lessons that he gave in Paris to the ubiquitous British ladies, despite his previous visit to London, despite his long friendship with Jane Stirling, at the end of the day he never learnt English, and it was now proving to be a considerable block to his social life.

Then came news of the 1848 Uprising in Poland, which filled him with anxiety for the family that he still had there. In July he attended a dinner with Polish emigrés at which he was able to talk Polish and politics and in his enthusiasm invited everyone to go back to his lodgings, where he played until two o'clock in the morning.

At the end of July the Queen left for Osborne, then Balmoral, and London emptied as Society followed her example, either going to their own estates in the country or taking the train to the North. The Queen travelled by boat, since she did not have much faith in the new trains, and Prince Albert had no choice but to follow — although he was invariably seasick.

Jane and Katherine also left for Scotland, but not without attempting to persuade Chopin to visit the land of their birth. They promised accommodation, hospitality, enthusiastic audiences and a warm Scottish welcome, not to mention clean air.

When they departed North Chopin found himself increasingly left to his own devices. It had been a good season, with hosts of virtuosi from all over Europe having taken the steamboat across the Channel. Berlioz eulogised that in no other country in the world was so much music consumed as during the London Season.

Now, suddenly, it was all over. The many interesting people Chopin had met during his three-month stay in the capital had largely disappeared, the lessons had tailed off, as had any prospects of concerts or soirées; and the expenses of his stay had whittled his capital down to £200.

He judged that he was going to need money desperately for the time when his health would finally collapse and he was no longer able to earn a living; Jane's offer sounded like a godsend. He decided to take it up and go to Scotland.

CHAPTER TWO

Edinburgh

Jane and Katherine joined the mass exodus from London at the end of July. Their brother-in-law, Lord Torphichen, who had already met Chopin in Paris, had written to him earlier that month inviting him to stay at Calder House, his home near Edinburgh. They now travelled to Scotland to make preparations for his visit.

Meanwhile, Henry Broadwood made the arrangements for his journey with his customary attention to detail and solicitude for Chopin's comfort. He booked three first-class seats on the London to Edinburgh train; one for Chopin, one for Daniel, and one for Chopin's feet, so that he could put them up when he was tired. It was the new, much improved West Coast route via Birmingham and Carlisle, which had only been opened that spring, and boasted comforts over and above those of the old eastern route, which necessitated a ferry and a transfer across the River Tweed on the border.

Being the very latest example of Victorian technology and enterprise, the new route was well subscribed by the wealthy landowners, who were now migrating in droves to their Scottish estates in time for the shooting and fishing.

Also on the train, at the instigation of Henry Broadwood, was John Muir Wood. He was the son of Andrew Wood, a music publisher in Edinburgh. A talented pianist, John studied with Kalkbrenner in Edinburgh, Pixis in Paris and Czerny in Vienna. Returning to Edinburgh in 1828 he at first earned his living as a music teacher until he went to London where he became involved in literary circles. In 1848 the family publishing firm opened a new branch in Glasgow, of which he became Director. The shops sold pianos, sheet music, musical instruments and theatre tickets. Chopin had once met him in Frankfurt. Since Muir Wood happened to be travelling to Scotland at about the same time as Chopin, Broadwood had suggested they should travel together on the same train, so that Muir Wood could keep an eye on the composer.

At 9 o'clock on the morning of Saturday, 5 August, the loose-coupled train started off out of Euston Station on its 400-mile journey north with a jerk that threw everyone off balance. By the time it reached its average speed of 40 miles per hour, the wind was whistling through the glassless windows and the luggage was bouncing around on the roof. With frequent halts for fuel and water, the train slowly chugged its way north, and it was a physically exhausted, stiff and battered Chopin who alighted at the haphazard collection of wooden shacks that still constituted Edinburgh's Lothian Road station, at 9 o'clock that same night. The grand design of the promised Italianate station was still on the drawing board, and was to remain there for the next half century before it was finally realised in bricks and mortar.

Among those who met the train was Dr Adam Lyszczynski, a Pole who had been part of the great emigration from his native land in the wake of the 1830–31 uprising. He settled in Edinburgh, studied at the medical school, and stayed on in the Scottish capital to build a career in homeopathic medicine. He married a young Scots girl, who gave him two children. He welcomed Chopin to Edinburgh in Polish, which he still spoke despite having become completely Scottish in his ways. Chopin was very touched by this, as any reference to his native land filled him with pleasure and nostalgia. He later wrote in Scotland: 'In a foreign

11

country it is the greatest comfort to have someone to take you back to the land of your birth whenever you look at them, speak or listen to them.'

Henry Broadwood had arranged rooms for Chopin at the Douglas Hotel (where Nos. 34–35 St Andrew Square stand today), to which Daniel had to carry the frail and exhausted composer.

Even first-class travel was an ordeal reserved for the fit and healthy in the nineteenth century.

On the next day, Sunday, 6 August, Chopin felt too weak to continue his journey to Calder House, and stayed in bed for the morning, with Daniel bringing him his morning chocolate and news of the weather.

It was a sunny day, and by noon Chopin had recovered enough to want to see the fine old city that lay awaiting him, particularly as Mrs Lyszczynski had promised to take him on a tour of the Scottish capital. By lunchtime, Chopin felt well enough to leave his bed, allowing Daniel to curl his hair, dress him and carry him down the stairs to where Mrs Lyszczynski was waiting at the front of the hotel. She had borrowed a carriage from a neighbour, and soon they were passing through the centre of what Chopin later described as 'this most handsome town'. Driving along Princes Street and looking up at the silhouetted castle on the skyline must have been as exciting and dramatic then as it is today, and although he was probably too weak to visit the castle he was driven along the Royal Mile to Holyrood House itself.

He made a point of visiting the magnificent memorial to Sir Walter Scott in East Princes Street Gardens. The monument had been erected two years previously, and besides, Chopin was an ardent admirer of Scott's work, and was thrilled to be visiting the city of his birth. He even bought a steel engraving of the monument to send to Poland. One can safely assume that he did not climb the 287 steps to the top in order to view the fine Georgian New Town.

The good clean Scottish air was already having a beneficial effect on Chopin's lungs, especially after the weeks spent in the polluted air of London, and on the following morning he felt well enough to take a walk round the environs of the Douglas Hotel, accompanied by the ever-watchful Daniel.

Muir Wood's father owned several music shops in Edinburgh and Chopin had promised to visit one that was close to the hotel. As he walked past the shop window at 12 Waterloo Place he heard the sound of one of his mazurkas being played on a piano, which was good theatre on the part of Muir Wood, who had set the situation up specially for Chopin. When he entered the shop he found that the pianist was blind; surely he would not have been able to resist playing the same mazurka himself, as a gentle tease to the blind man? In later years Muir Wood's own son used to boast that Chopin and his father had played a duet together, probably on this occasion.

Later that morning Chopin bought some prints of Edinburgh, but he was not pleased with them. He did not consider that they did justice to a very beautiful city, and was disappointed that the only views he could find to send to his family in Poland were 'horrible', and he complained that he could not find any 'prettier ones'.

Taking all things into consideration, however, it had been a good morning, and Chopin returned to the Douglas Hotel for lunch with a lighter heart than he had had for weeks. He liked what he had seen so far of Scotland; the people were kind and the air was clean. Moreover, he had stopped coughing and spitting blood, and when the carriage drew up at the Douglas Hotel that afternoon to take him to Calder

House, he was ready. With the driver seated on the lead horse, Chopin climbed in and the carriage set off on the fifteen-mile trip to Calder House. It was a sunny day, and the journey in the luxurious carriage was comfortable and smooth.

The approach to the old manor house was impressive, through a vast park full of old trees and large lawned areas.

The carriage bearing the composer came to the end of the long drive and drew up in front of the entrance, where Lord Torphichen, Jane and Katherine were all there to greet him.

Lord Torphichen, delighted to have Chopin as a guest in his stately home, was ready to go out of his way to show him the meaning of Scottish hospitality, and to make the musician as welcome and as comfortable as possible.

As he was helped out of the carriage by his faithful valet and welcomed warmly and kindly by his host, Chopin felt that his journey to Scotland had been a very good idea.

CHAPTER THREE

Calder House

Chopin described Calder House as an old manor with walls eight feet thick. There were many staircases, countless large and airy rooms, galleries and long corridors full of portraits of past members of the family: the men dressed in kilts or armour, and the women dressed in farthingales. The very fabric of the house exuded a rich air of history which delighted the romantic soul of Chopin. John Knox had celebrated communion there for the first time in 1556, in the room below the one now given to the composer. The house also claimed a red-capped ghost that reputedly walked at midnight, although Chopin was to be disappointed in his efforts to see it; it did not appear during his stay.

Chopin was very close to his family in Poland, and stayed in constant touch with them throughout his life. He wrote to them from Calder House, describing the beautiful room he had been given, and the fine view from his window that overlooked the extensive grounds and the centuries-old trees.

He enjoyed the attention of servants, the elegant furniture, the well-stocked library, the ready availability of carriages and horses whenever he wanted to go for a drive, and the plentiful supply of good food, as well as a morning cup of his favourite hot chocolate. Henry Broadwood had installed a piano in his room, and Jane had also brought a Pleyel piano — as favoured by Chopin — up from London, and had placed it in the drawing room. Everything that could be done for his comfort had been foreseen and provided, and he was treated as an honoured guest. 'My worthy

Scots!' he wrote, 'I cannot think of anything which isn't immediately realised.'

James Sandilands was born in 1770 and inherited the title of Lord Torphichen on the death of his father in 1815. Always a strong and virile man, in his youth he had captained an East Indiaman. In 1806 he married Margaret Stirling, one of Jane's elder sisters, who bore him one daughter. When Margaret died in Paris in 1836, Jane and Katherine, who were very fond of their elderly and still very active brother-in-law, made Calder House their Scottish home base.

Lord Torphichen liked and admired Chopin, extended his invitation for the whole summer, and even asked him to come back the following year. Such hospitality was overwhelming for the sick musician.

As in most country houses, there was a constant turnover of house guests, most of them up for the season. Like the rest of them, Chopin breakfasted in his room, where Daniel, as usual, would curl his hair, dress him, and prepare him for the day. Lunch was at two o'clock, with the afternoon free for drives in the countryside, visiting neighbours, or just walking in the extensive grounds. He particularly enjoyed strolling around the ornamental lake, and commented on how the sound of the water carried melodies.

One of the visitors to Calder House during Chopin's stay was his former pupil and friend, Thomas Tellefsen. He was born in Trondheim, Norway, in 1823, and went to Paris to pursue his musical studies with Kalkbrenner and Chopin. He was particularly influenced by the latter, and emulated his style both in his delicate touch at the piano, and in his piano compositions, which, like his role model's, included mazurkas, waltzes, nocturnes and a couple of piano concertos. His Chopinesque style, both in composition and execution, won him considerable acclaim during the middle years of the century, especially as an interpreter of Chopin. But his own compositions lacked the chromatic inventiveness and inspired cohesion of his master; consequently Time was to be his judge, and his music has all but faded into oblivion.

Tellefsen had preceded Chopin in their flight from Paris to London, and he had already begun to establish himself as an important young performer and teacher in the English capital. When Chopin followed, Tellefsen was in a position to show his former master some of the London scene, and Chopin was obviously very pleased to see his young friend once again under yet another set of circumstances.

Another visitor to Calder House was Dr Lyszczynski, who was the Stirling family's homeopathic physician. Bonded by both language and nationality, he and Chopin had struck up a warm friendship, and the doctor now offered him an open invitation to his Edinburgh house. Ever hungry for Polish company and conversation, Chopin took up this offer several times.

The Calder estate included a dairy farm, which Chopin regularly visited. His comments on the local cows — he had never seen highland cattle before — their 'fierce expressions', and the rich butter and cream that they produced, were almost naïve in their simplicity, and reflect a childlike delight in all things rural. 'This innocence of nature brought back to me my feelings as a child,' he once wrote. Chopin was urban as well as urbane, a city sophisticate more at home in salons and cafés than in fields and meadows. And yet, the simple delights of the Scottish countryside reminded him of his birthplace among the Mazovian farms near Warsaw. His long walks in the grounds of Calder House made those remote memories of a happy childhood come flooding back.

Fryderyk Franciszek Chopin was born, according to legend, to the sound of the village band celebrating a local peasant wedding, on the evening of 1 March 1810. Nicholas and Justyna Chopin, already the parents of three-year-old Ludwika, lived in a small, whitewashed, thatched cottage in Żelazowa Wola, the estate of Count Skarbek, a distant cousin of Justyna's. She was governess and piano teacher to the Skarbeks' five children, while Nicholas, a teacher by profession, was their tutor.

Soon after Fryderyk was born, the Chopins moved to Warsaw where French-born Nicholas had found a post as French teacher at the Lyceum.

In his formative years in Warsaw, Chopin developed the unique duality of nationality which was to become his hallmark in the years to come. The soul of his music was essentially Polish, yet its outward expression owed a debt to French elegance, refinement and culture; and the heady atmosphere of the Paris of Louis-Philippe acted as a perfect outlet for his art.

The Chopins' apartment in the school buildings was always full of music and merriment, for Nicholas welcomed visitors, and at their frequent gatherings Justyna would play the piano for dancing. Fryderyk loved these parties, and would sit entranced by the sound of the piano. There was a family in-joke that bad piano playing made him scream with displeasure.

Nicholas enjoyed music, although he was not very good at it. So as not to be left out, he tried to learn the flute, but little Fryderyk broke it. Perhaps, continued the family in-joke, Fryderyk did not like his flute playing either!

Apocrypha learned at his mother's knee, maybe, but the underlying trait stayed with him for the rest of his life. For Chopin only the best was good enough. He would not be satisfied with a composition until he had tempered and honed it to perfection. He learned by the sweat of his brow how hard and painstaking it was to make his music sound spontaneous and improvised. Then, he would suffer no tampering with the finished article, even down to the last carefully weighed dynamic.

The foundations for Chopin's pianistic technique lay with Wojciech Żywny, his first piano teacher, enlisted when Justyna decided that the six-year-old Fryderyk needed more professional attention than she was able to give him. Żywny was an excellent teacher, and Fryderyk a responsive pupil. The old man introduced him to the elegance of Mozart and the technical demands of J. S. Bach, and under his tutelage Chopin developed his singularly delicate touch, and the seemingly effortless technical skill which were prominent features of his Scottish performances.

Life was good at the Lyceum, and the Chopins soon had two more girls, Izabella and Emilia. However, none of the children enjoyed good health; they were anaemic, suffered from constant colds, and regularly fell victim to infection.

When Fryderyk was five, he was too young to understand the changes sweeping Europe in the wake of the defeat of Napoleon, but as he grew older a fierce patriotism dominated his life and music. Events in Poland were always of supreme interest to him, and possibly at no time more so than during 1848, the year of the Poznań Uprising. While in Scotland, he was avid for news of his native land, and the effect of the troubles on his family. Refugees were flooding to Paris, London and Edinburgh with tales of merciless repression and cruel atrocities against Poles on the part of both Russians and Prussians.

The nineteenth century had not been kind to Poland. After several centuries of rich and often enlightened history, the nation was dismantled and partitioned in three stages by Russia, Prussia and Austria. In 1795 Poland ceased to exist.

The Duchy of Warsaw, where Chopin was born, was a creation of Napoleon's political machinations. It gave Poland nominal independence, the Napoleonic code, and some pretence at self-determination, in return for allegiance. In 1815, after the defeat of Napoleon, the Congress of Vienna created, and enlarged, the so-called Congress Kingdom of Poland out of the remnants of Napoleon's puppet state. The new King of Poland was the intelligent but volatile Tsar Alexander I of Russia, who wanted to give the Poles the freedom to express their nationality, but within the framework of Russian rule.

Alexander appointed his brother, the ugly, bad-tempered, unenlightened but basically well-meaning Grand Duke Constantine as Commander of the Polish Garrison in Warsaw. His savage outbursts would bring terror to the hearts of the Poles, but Chopin recalled his first meeting with the 'Wolf-man' with wry amusement. Ever since his first concert at the Radziwiłł Palace two days after his eighth birthday, Fryderyk was much talked about throughout Warsaw, and he received many invitations to the homes of the aristocracy. It was only a matter of time before Constantine invited this amazing little Polish boy to play for him.

Fryderyk's nervousness at playing for the fearsome Duke soon disappeared. While he played the

Duke listened intently, but when Fryderyk began to improvise a march, Constantine leapt up from his chair and marched round the room in time to the music, swinging his arms and grinning with sheer delight. He then decreed that Fryderyk's march (now lost) be played at all military reviews!

After that Fryderyk was often seen at the Palace, where the whisper was that he was the only person alive able to sedate the Grand Duke Constantine out of his frequent temper tantrums. As Fryderyk's music became more mature, the Grand Duke no longer strutted up and down, but sat beside him at the piano and listened.

When he was thirteen, the Chopins spent an idyllic summer holiday at Żelazowa Wola with the Skarbeks, and Fryderyk took every opportunity to play the piano and give recitals for the Skarbeks and their guests. The piano was hauled out into the garden and placed under the linden trees, and every evening Fryderyk would play to the family, and to the villagers who crept up to listen.

That autumn, back in Warsaw, Fryderyk became a pupil at the Lyceum, where he built up a reputation not only for his music, but also for his easy wit and his ability to tell outrageous stories while seated at the piano, supplying his own background music.

In Paris, Chopin was renowned as a witty dinner-table conversationalist and raconteur — a talent he was now unable to utilise because of his lack of English.

In spite of the friendly company, dinner at Calder House was an ordeal for Chopin. Served at seven, it was a long-drawn out ceremony, with many courses and varied drinks, with the women retreating at about nine to the drawing-room, leaving a bewildered Chopin trying to converse with non-French-speaking men, who primarily wanted to talk about shooting rather than music. As Chopin now drank very little the masculine routine of port and cigars held no attraction for him, and he found the long evenings at the table very wearing.

What Chopin made of the Stirling's favourite family toast is not recorded: 'Here's to our folk and your folk and all the folk that likes our folk and your folk and if folk would let folk, folk would like folk better than folk ever did like folk since folk was folk'!

After dinner they would go through to the drawing-room, where the company, especially the ladies, were naturally keen to hear Chopin play. By this time of the evening, Chopin would be tired, with his lungs smarting from the effects of cigar smoke; so the nightly recitals became an ordeal which through courtesy to both host and guests he was unable to refuse. Jane in particular wanted to display to all present 'her' elegant little musician, and these musical soirées were the perfect expression of her supreme joy and pride.

Chopin's weakness now prevented him from playing any of his larger-scale works; the sonatas, the polonaises and the Fantasia were out of the question, not only on account of their length, but also because of the considerable physical demands involved. However, the candle-lit country drawing-room, with its rich drapery and elegant furniture bedecked with ornate vases filled with late summer flowers, as well as Jane's Pleyel grand piano, provided the perfect romantic setting for the waltzes, the mazurkas, and particularly the supremely light-weight Berceuse. Naturally, no soirée would have been complete without the two nocturnes that Chopin had dedicated to Jane.

When eventually the evenings came to a close it was an exhausted Chopin that would be carried upstairs by Daniel and put to bed.

While in his teens, Fryderyk spent a lot of time with his little sister Emilia, who was bedridden with the same tuberculosis which was now ravaging his lungs. They both shared a love of poetry and stories, and the two of them formed a 'Literary Entertainment Society', with Fryderyk the president, Emilia the secretary, and the Lyceum pupils who boarded with the Chopins the members. The society's aims were to exchange stories and poems.

Fryderyk was very supportive of Emilia, and loved her dearly. But since his own health was also deteriorating, Nicholas sent him on holiday to Szafarnia, near Toruń, where he was put on a strict diet, with lots of fresh air and exercise. On one occasion his best friend from the Lyceum, Julian Fontana, went with him, and together they went riding, walking — and hunting for girls! Julian remained one of his closest friends for the rest of his life.

While at Calder House, Chopin was overjoyed to hear from Julian, who had just arrived in London from America.

'If only I were better,' Chopin immediately replied, 'I would travel to London tomorrow just to give you a hug … I can hardly breathe: I am just about ready to expire.' But he still managed to retain his sense of humour: 'All I have left is a long nose and a fourth finger out of practice,' he continued.

It was twenty years since his childhood ended with the death of Emilia, aged fourteen, from tuberculosis.

Now, in the idyllic pastoral surroundings of Calder House, the knowledge that it was just a matter of time before his own turn came, weighed heavily on his mind.

When there were no guests at Calder House, Chopin spent his time in the company of Lord Torphichen. 'In the evenings I play Scottish melodies to the kind old lord,' he wrote, 'while he sings along and does his best to express his feelings to me in French.' The two men spent many happy hours exchanging folk tunes and dances, each in his own way. As well as listening to Lord Torphichen humming tunes at the piano, Chopin also managed to hear some 'pretty Scotch airs' sung and played by the local villagers. However, nothing that he heard in Scotland inspired him to write.

His three Ecossaises were composed years before in Paris, and their debt to Scottish folk music was purely circumstantial. Chopin was interested in ethnic music in general. His Bolero and Tarantella, as well as the Ecossaises, bear witness to this; but it was form and rhythmic pattern that intrigued him, rather than true ethnic feel.

For Jane Stirling the two-and-a-half idyllic weeks that Chopin spent at Calder was a truly memorable period in her life, and she luxuriated in the close contact that she was able to have with the man that she so patently, and at the end of the day, so pathetically, adored.

Jane's ideas of patronage included a closer, more romantic relationship than Chopin was prepared to be involved in, and the fact was becoming increasingly obvious. She was now 44, six year Chopin's senior, and pictures show that time had not been kind to her. But she was wealthy enough to indulge her fancies, and with her many relations in the Scottish Lowlands, she was able to take the weakening Chopin on a constant and gruelling round of family homes; and Chopin's natural

A photograph of Chopin, after a Daguerrotype (*Courtesy of the Royal College of Music, London*).

The Douglas Hotel, Edinburgh, where Henry Broadwood booked rooms for Chopin. Nos. 34–35 St Andrew Square now occupy the site (*Courtesy of Central Library, Edinburgh*).

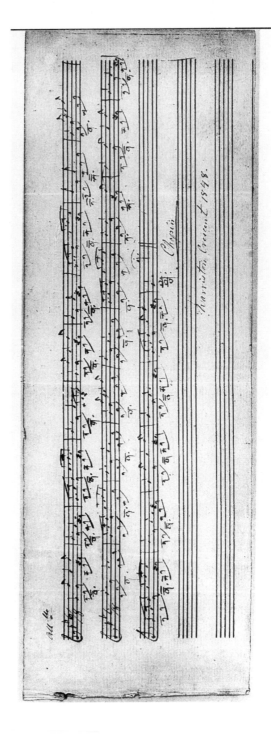

The manuscript of Chopin's song 'Wiosna' (Spring), written at 48 Warriston Crescent, Edinburgh (*Courtesy of the Biblioteka Kornicka, Kornick, Poland*).

A rare picture of Wishaw House, from an early postcard.

Calder House, a stately manor near Edinburgh, where Chopin stayed as the guest of Lord Torphichen (*Courtesy of Lord and Lady Torphichen*).

Johnstone Castle, which was demolished by the local council after the Second World War and replaced by a housing estate. One tower of the castle still survives.

Strachur House, overlooking the Strachur Bay on Loch Fyne, where Chopin spent a week as the guest of Lord and Lady Murray (*Courtesy of Sir Fitzroy Maclean, Bart.*).

The Merchants' Hall, Glasgow, now Hutcheson's Hall, the regional headquarters of the National Trust for Scotland at 158 Ingram Street (*Courtesy of the National Trust for Scotland*).

Gargunnock House, once the property of Jane Stirling's brother, Charles.

Keir House, near Dunblane. Chopin declared that he would like to live there.

Chopin stayed with the Duke and Duchess of Hamilton at Hamilton Palace, demolished in the 1920s. This is the Mausoleum, the only remaining building on the estate.

Marie Wodzinska
(*Collection Edouard Ganche*).

George Sand
(*From the crayon portrait by
Thomas Couture*).

Jane Stirling. Portrait by Deveria
(*Collection Edouard Ganche*).

Princess Marcelina Czartoryska.

Milliken House, Renfrewshire, where Chopin was the guest of Sir William Napier, the husband of Eliza, Jane Stirling's sister (*Courtesy of Mrs Valerie McIntyre, White House of Milliken*).

A late drawing of Chopin by Kwiatowski (*Courtesy of the University of Edinburgh Library*).

courtesy made it impossible for him to decline. That she meant well is not in doubt, but her growing obsession with the composer blinded her to the impossible burden that the visits were placing on a dying man.

Meanwhile, Chopin was already considering his bleak future and the desperate need to make some money, not only for living expenses, but also as a buttress against the possibility of a long and terminal decline. Deep down, he had few illusions about the nature of his illness, and the halcyon days at Calder, while so agreeable and peaceful in some ways, nevertheless gave him time to reflect on the dark cloud that hung over his future.

He still had his apartment in Paris, let while he was abroad, and although he was very happy in Scotland, he dreamed of returning soon to the scene of his past triumphs.

In the meantime, Muir Wood had not been inactive in his capacity as concert promoter. 'They want me to play in Edinburgh at the beginning of October,' wrote Chopin. 'If I shall make some money, and if I have the strength, I shall certainly do it, for I don't know how I am going to manage this winter.'

Nor had Henry Broadwood been idle. He had arranged a concert for 28 August in Manchester, eight hours by train from Edinburgh. So Chopin took up Dr Lyszczynski's offer of hospitality, and invited himself to his house at 10 Warriston Crescent, for a couple of days of homeopathic treatment, as the first stage of his journey to Manchester.

The grey, stone-built terraced houses of Warriston Crescent are described in a contemporary guide to Edinburgh as:

> A neat row of moderately sized houses which would be very pleasant residences were it not

for the foetid odours arising from the filth which is most disgracefully allowed to accumulate from a large common sewer emptying itself into the bed of the river [Leith] immediately behind the houses, the sludge from which is allowed to stagnate and ferment almost literally beneath the windows, to the scandal of the public authorities and the infinite disgust of every passer-by.

Fortunately for Chopin, he was given the nursery at the front of the house overlooking the street, with Daniel occupying a little room next door. The Lyszczynski children were sent to stay with a neighbour.

Dr Lyszczynski's wife was musical, and there was a small Broadwood piano in the drawing-room downstairs, which she played. During his short stay Chopin would sit down at the piano after dinner and play to her and her husband, and friends who dropped in. Sometimes Mrs Lyszczynski would sing while Chopin accompanied her; on one occasion she declined to sing and Chopin, astonished and a little angry, said to her husband, 'Doctor! Would you take it amiss if I were to force your wife to do it?'

At the end of the evening the Doctor himself would carry Chopin up the winding staircase to the nursery, where Daniel would undress him, and put him to bed.

Chopin was now becoming irritable and increasingly frail, and everything had to be done for him. The doctor's homeopathic treatment proved effective, and during his stay Chopin recovered somewhat. What was more the informal atmosphere of a 'Polish' house, without the hassle of language barriers, had done Chopin a power of good, if only psychologically.

On Friday 25 August Daniel and Jane took a somewhat revitalised Chopin to the station to catch the train for Manchester.

CHAPTER FOUR

Manchester

Salis Schwabe was a rich German Jew and Protestant convert, who had emigrated to Glasgow in 1817, and moved to Manchester in 1832. He made a fortune in manufacturing and bought Crumpsall House, well outside the foul, smoky atmosphere of the heavily industrialised city. He was a cultured music lover who played both the piano and the organ, and it was said he played with 'delicacy and sentiment'. He had many musical friends, among them Jane Stirling, Jenny Lind, the 'Swedish Nightingale', and the briefly-famed composer, Sigismund Neukomm, who had been taught by Haydn and was known to Chopin. His wife Julie was an educated and intelligent woman who spent a great deal of time travelling abroad with the radical politician and economist, Richard Cobden, and later wrote of their travels in both French and English.

Salis Schwabe had already met Chopin in Paris and, together with his wife, was delighted to accede to Jane's request and have Chopin as a guest at their home while he played in the concert.

Crumpsall House was a square Georgian mansion with an imposing entrance and large, airy rooms that let light flood in through their big windows. It was situated at the end of a long drive in a park that boasted fine, landscaped gardens with flower beds, many trees and lawns, a rose garden with a sundial and an ornamental lake.

The house was demolished in 1934 to make way for a housing estate.

Chopin and his entourage caught the 10.30 a.m. train from Edinburgh on Friday 25 August, to allow him time to recover from the journey before the concert. They arrived at Salford Station in New Bailey Street, which today looks exactly as it looked then, and by the time that they arrived at Crumpsall House, Chopin had been travelling for eight hours.

There was no question of him joining the company at dinner that evening. Daniel put him straight to bed, and there he stayed for the next twenty-four hours, building up such strength as he would need for the concert.

By the Saturday evening he was able to join his hosts at dinner, and most probably would have played for them afterwards. There had been many occasions when Chopin had been expected to play after dinner, if only as a matter of form; but he found playing to the unenlightened extremely tedious; the Salis Schwabes were not importunate people, and would not have expected a performance in return for hospitality, as would be the unwritten law in many houses. Jenny Lind recalled one occasion when they deliberately put the piano in another room so as not to force her into singing for them — although of course she insisted on doing so in the end. Chopin would have found such an informed and cultured audience irresistible, and would have been very happy to give a recital for those who would genuinely appreciate his art.

The concert was held on 28 August in the Gentlemen's Concert Hall, before 1,200 people, the largest audience that Chopin had ever performed to. In fact, it proved too large for his now very delicate playing, and although he was paid a welcome £60, the concert was not really a great success for him.

Chopin was only one of the performers at this concert; a close friend, George Osborne, was scheduled to accompany other artists on the programme. He was an Irish pianist who had been taught in Paris by Kalkbrenner and Pixis, and now lived in London. Chopin did not want him to be there when he played, for he knew that his performance would be lost in the large hall.

'My dear Osborne, you who have heard me playing in Paris,' he said 'my playing will be lost in such a large room, and my compositions ineffective. You being there will cause pain to both you and me.'

Osborne agreed to go out for Chopin's items, but secretly crept back and was very distressed at the performance.

'I was there, in a corner,' he wrote. 'I helped to cheer him, but his playing was too delicate and I was so sorry for him.'

The other performers were all singers who were received with greater enthusiasm than was Chopin. The following Wednesday the *Manchester Guardian* reviewed the concert, describing his playing as 'the perfection of chamber music — fit to be associated with the most refined instrumental quartets ... but wanting breadth and obviousness of design and executive power to be effective in a large concert hall.'

Other critics were more enthusiastic, and the *Manchester Courier* reported:

> We can, with great sincerity, say that he delighted us, though we did not discover in him the vigour of a Thalberg. Yet there was a chasteness and purity of style, a correctness of manipulation, combined with a brilliancy of touch, and a delicate sensibility of expression which we have never heard excelled. He played in the second act Nocturnes, Etudes and Berceuse and elicited a rapturous encore. He did not, however, repeat any part, but treated the audience with what appeared to be a fragment of

great beauty. The room was filled to overflowing by a most brilliant audience.

After the concert Chopin stayed for a while with the Salis Schwabes to recuperate. He spent a few peaceful days walking in the grounds, admiring the lake and enjoying the warm, late summer sunshine; Jane probably accompanied him on his walks, no doubt feeding her ever-growing delusions that she might yet elicit a stronger emotional response from her beloved master. Nothing further is known about his stay with the Salis Schwabes, since he did not write to anyone from Crumpsall House, preferring to confine his thoughts to himself. The concert reinforced in his troubled soul the fact that he was now in serious decline, both physically and musically. He was well aware of his shortcomings in a concert hall, and the prospect of the projected Edinburgh concert in October was now weighing heavily on his mind.

The attentions of Jane Stirling were by now becoming oppressive, but he was too polite — and helpless — to do anything about them.

The exact date of his return to Scotland is not known, but back in Edinburgh he again stayed with the Lyszczynskis for one night before travelling on to Johnstone Castle, just outside Glasgow, on Saturday 2 September.

CHAPTER FIVE

Johnstone Castle

Johnstone Castle, 11 miles to the west of Glasgow was largely demolished in 1950, and now consists of just one preserved tower surrounded by a modern housing estate in the town of Johnstone. When Chopin visited it, he described it as 'fine and luxurious, and maintained on a grand scale'. At the time it was the property of Ludovic Houston, the husband of Anne, Jane's 65 year-old elder sister. At Jane's instigation, she had invited Chopin to stay at the castle as part of the grand tour of her relatives; Chopin grew to like Anne Houston very much.

But despite the attentions and hospitality lavished on him by Anne Houston, Katherine Erksine — and of course, Jane — Chopin had become bored as well as irritated by the constant demands on his art, his emotions and his presence. The weather had deteriorated, and the warm sunshine was replaced by rain and mist, melancholy harbingers of the Scottish autumn to come. The restful walks in the grounds, which Chopin loved so much, had to stop, and the only amusements left to him were visiting Jane's friends and relations, of whom she was able to produce legions. As time went on, he found her attention, and assumption of rights to which she was not entitled, stifling.

'The weather has changed, and it is dreadful outside. I am feeling sick and depressed, and everyone wears me down with their excessive attentions. I cannot breathe and I cannot work. I feel alone, alone, alone, even though I am surrounded by people,' he wrote to his friend Grzymała.

Chopin became very lonely at Johnstone. He missed those warm friendships of his halcyon days in Paris, especially that of his fellow countryman Grzymała, whose extraordinary and action-packed career had spanned the length of Europe and had come to such grief the previous year.

Wojciech Grzymała was born at Dunajowice in Podolia in 1793. He held various military posts both in the Duchy of Warsaw and the Congress Kingdom. In 1812, with the rout of Napoleon's army, he was taken prisoner of war by the Russians. After the creation of the Congress Kingdom, he continued to serve under Grand Duke Constantine.

In 1825 he was involved, along with a cabal of Polish officers, in the Decembrists' plot to place Constantine on the Russian throne after the death of Tsar Alexander I. The plot failed, Nicholas I became tsar, hanged the five ringleaders, and imprisoned the rest, including Grzymała. The affair made Nicholas ever suspicious of Poles, which made his regime far more unpopular than that of his predecessor, and led to the ill-fated uprisings of 1830 and 1848.

Grzymała was a skilled financial manipulator. He was released from prison, and in 1830, as an official in the Polish treasury, he was sent on a diplomatic mission to Berlin, Paris and London to negotiate a loan for the Bank of Poland. He stayed in London for two years before going to Paris, where he decided to stay for good.

His devastating good looks, charm, wit and culture, as well as his virtuosity at the Bourse, enabled him to live extremely well, and patronise all the best salons. Wealth, society and beautiful women

*were always at his fingertips. He counted most of
the French capital's artists, writers and musicians
among his close friends, and dined out frequently
on tales of his many adventures.*

*His friends included George Sand in her own
right, Chopin himself, as well as the Czartoryskis,
with whom he was in the vanguard of moral and
financial support for the Polish refugees and émigré
community. Chopin and Grzymała had both been
frequent visitors to the Czartoryskis' suite at the Hotel
Lambert on the Ile St Louis, which was at the time the
epicentre of the Polish scene in Paris.*

*To Chopin Grzymała was a special friend, men-
tor and recipient of many of his letters and most
intimate confidences.*

*After Chopin's break with George Sand,
Grzymała sided with the composer, and that
same year lost a fortune on the Bourse, which
was an added burden for Chopin's troubled mind.
Wojciech Grzymała died in 1871.*

Now, languishing under the dark clouds that hung
over Johnstone Castle, Chopin had also come to the
inescapable conclusion that he was burnt-out as a
composer as well as a performer. Jane provided pianos,
music and paper, but the inspiration was missing.
During his time in Scotland Chopin composed no
significant music, apart from the recently discovered
'Spring', and this fact preyed heavily on his mind.

Chopin had one very near brush with death when
driving in a coupé on his way to pay a visit to some
neighbours. One of the two English thoroughbred
horses reared suddenly, and started to bolt. They
were on a downward slope and the coachman was
unable to control the horses; the reins broke and he
was thrown clear. Daniel jumped out of the coach as

it careered wildly and hit a tree on the edge of a steep drop. The coach shattered into pieces, with Chopin still inside it. One of the horses broke loose and bolted, while the other fell on to the stricken coach.

The drama was watched from a distance by some local people who rushed to the scene expecting to find everyone inside dead, but to their amazement they found Chopin crawling gingerly out of the wreckage, bruised, cut and very shaken, but otherwise unhurt.

Writing about the incident he said that he was completely calm as he saw what he was convinced was his last hour approaching; but in retrospect he was appalled by what might have been. Broken legs would have been bad enough, but were his hands to have been damaged, it would have been a tragedy.

On a lighter note, he found the Scottish obsession with family connections rather ludicrous, and related with amusement the pride of one woman who claimed to be the thirteenth cousin of Mary, Queen of Scots, and had retained the surname Stuart when she married, with her husband's approval. Chopin was bewildered by the detailed tracing of kinship and wryly recounted: 'Here they are all cousins related to great families with names that no one on the Continent has ever heard of. Conversation is entirely genealogical, just like in the Gospels: who begat whom, whom he begat, and whom he begat ... and so on for two pages all the way back to Jesus.'

The weather worsened and thunder and hail beat down on the grouse moors. The hardy younger members of the house-party nevertheless went out shooting, leaving Chopin with 'a motley crowd of ladies and seventy- to eighty-year-old lords, but no young people'. And Jane.

Chopin would gladly have left Johnstone Castle but for the fact that Muir Wood had set up a concert for him at the Merchant's Hall in Glasgow on 27 September. For this he sold tickets from his Glasgow music shop at 42 Buchanan Street. Priced at half-a-guinea each they were the most expensive concert tickets ever sold in that city up till then!

As part of his tour of Jane's relatives, Chopin went to stay at Milliken House, the home of Sir William Napier, the husband of Eliza Stirling, the fifth daughter of John Stirling, another of Jane's sisters. The House, in Milliken Park, was within easy driving distance of Johnstone Castle. It was demolished in the 1920s, and some of the stones were used to build an extension to the 'White House of Milliken', a private residence situated just outside Brookfield.

Muir Wood visited Chopin both at Johnstone Castle and at Milliken House. He had great difficulty with the concert arrangements because Chopin kept changing his mind about the programme. Muir Wood found himself chasing Chopin round the countryside in a desperate effort to confirm the items of the programme, and had to return several times to verify Chopin's decisions. After the traumas of the Manchester concert, when Chopin withdrew the 'Ballade in A flat' from the programme at the very last moment, fearful that he would not be able to do justice to its weightier sections, he was now juggling with some basic decisions: would he dare include some of his heavier works, or would he stick to the tried, tested and essentially delicate ones?

At sometime Chopin probably went to nearvy Glentyan House, owned by Jane's elder brother James, who had bought it during the first quarter of the nineteenth century, but no details are known.

During his sojourn at Johnstone Castle, a promised stay with Lord and Lady Murray at Strachur was threatened by the bad weather: 'It is impossible to go out as it has been raining and windy for several days. I don't know what to do about my trip to Strachur. One has to cross Loch Long, one of the most beautiful lochs, and sail along the west coast of Scotland. It is only four hours away.'

Lady Murray was a pianist who had been taught by Chopin in London. She had teamed up and played duets with Louis Dreschler, a cellist and pupil of Chopin's friend, Auguste Franchomme. Chopin met Dreschler in London, and again in Edinburgh. Writing about the meetings to Franchomme, Chopin said: 'Dreschler appeared to me a fine young fellow, and loves you much. He plays duets with a great lady of this country, Lady Murray, one of my sexagenarian pupils in London, to whom I have also promised a visit in her beautiful mansion.' Her husband, John Archibald, Lord Murray, was a judge and sometime MP for Leith.

Despite the weather, Chopin kept his promise and spent a week at Strachur House overlooking the Strachur Bay on Loch Fyne. In the event, the weather improved and there was an Indian Summer that enabled him to go for walks in the grounds of the house and along the pebbly beach of the bay. He even went for a trip in the little Loch Fyne steamer. He relished the local fare, herrings and salmon from the loch, grouse pies, venison, and all the good wholesome foods to be found during a Scottish autumn.

A contemporary traveller described a breakfast of fresh herrings as 'the newest herrings are swimming about all alive at nine o'clock in the morning, and at a quarter past nine are served up fried with the coffee.'

Dinner-times still presented problems, with the long smoky evenings spent listening to hunting and fishing talk in English; but at least he was eating what they caught, which was some consolation!

Jane was not a member of this house-party; however, her place was taken by several other admiring women.

Chopin was gallant to all ladies alike, and of course he was expected to play the piano every evening. Whether or not he obliged as a matter of form, he knew that his hostess's interest was genuine.

Or was it? It was Lady Murray herself who shattered Chopin's faith in her sense of good taste one evening after he had played the piano to the assembled company. She sent for a concertina, and proceeded to play on it what he described as the most dreadful tunes. When he looked at her face expecting to see that she was teasing him he was appalled to see that she was being serious. 'But what would you expect?' he asked Grzymała in a letter. 'Everyone here appears to have a screw loose!'

Chopin returned to Johnstone Castle on Saturday, 23 August to prepare for the Glasgow concert and found a letter waiting for him from Prince Aleksander Czartoryski, the nephew of Prince Adam Czartoryski. The letter contained the welcome news that he was in Edinburgh with his wife Marcelina and their young son, Marcel, all of whom were very anxious to see him.

Without further ado, and despite any protests about his tiredness after his journey back from Strachur, Chopin had himself driven back to the station, and 'jumped into the train' to Edinburgh.

CHAPTER SIX

Glasgow

Princess Marcelina Czartoryska was born into the eminent Polish/Lithuanian Radziwill family in 1817. As well as being a talented musician, she was beautiful, intelligent and vivacious. She attracted the attention of Prince Aleksander Czartoryski, the nephew of Prince Adam Czartoryski, who, as President of the Hotel Lambert organised in Paris, was in effect 'pretender' to the Polish throne. They married in Vienna.

Educated firstly in Vienna, where she studied piano with Beethoven's teacher, Carl Czerny, in 1845 she went to Paris where she became Chopin's pupil. Under his tutorship she went from strength to strength, and within a short time had established herself as one of the finest and most faithful interpreters of his music. Berlioz heard her playing, and in his *Memoirs* judged her to be 'a musician of wide knowledge and exemplary taste, and a distinguished pianist'.

As a member of the aristocracy she defied social convention by performing in public. Her name was musically linked to those of Liszt, Vieuxtemps and Franchomme, among many other musicians; she was also the centre of intellectual and artistic circles in Paris and Kraków, where she eventually settled. She spent the latter years of her life giving concerts throughout Poland, in which she not only played Chopin, but also the works of other, lesser-known Polish composers, such as Gomólka and Żeleński.

She remained Chopin's good friend and patroness for the rest of his life and was at his bedside when he died.

Now, having fallen victim to Austrian power politics, she had been expelled from Vienna as a Russian subject, and had come to Edinburgh with her husband and young son Marcel.

On reaching Edinburgh Chopin went straight to the Czartoryskis and spent several hours in their company. His spirits revived, as they always did when he had a chance to speak Polish and hear the latest news from Poland and Vienna. He was also very taken by little Marcel whom he described as 'a fine boy. He can sing my music, and if anyone plays it wrongly he sings the music to show them the right way.'

Having secured their promise that they would travel to Glasgow for his concert, Chopin left the Czartoryskis and took a carriage to Warriston Crescent, where he stayed overnight with the Lyszczynskis.

There were no trains on Sunday, and he returned to Johnstone Castle the following Monday morning to prepare for the concert on the Wednesday afternoon.

On the morning of the big day, Chopin, Jane and Anne Houston left Johnstone Castle in a carriage for Hutcheson Street in Glasgow. Muir Wood and Jane had done an excellent job; the Merchants' Hall was packed with the aristocracy and friends who had come from all over Scotland to support the famous composer.

Bills that had gone out previously announced that the concert was under the patronage of:

> The Duchess of Argyll
> The Countess of Eglinton and Winton
> The Countess of Glasgow
> The Countess of Cathcart
> Lady Isabella Gordon
> The Baroness Sempill
> The Lady Blantyre

The Lady Belhaven
The Hon Mrs Speirs of Elderslie
The Hon Mrs Colquhoun etc, etc.

Lord and Lady Murray had driven down from Strachur, Lord Torphichen had travelled across from Calder, Prince and Princess Czartoryski were there with young Marcel, the Duke and Duchess of Hamilton attended, as did all the Stirling clan who were in the vicinity, and Dr and Mrs Lyszczynski came across from Edinburgh with a group of the friends who had attended their evening soirées.

Surveying the Hall Muir Wood felt both satisfied with the attendance and relieved that Chopin had arrived to perform; there were times in the past weeks when he had wondered if it would all come together.

PROGRAMME
of
M. CHOPIN'S MATINEE MUSICALE
Merchants' Hall
Sept 27, 1848

---

1. Piano-forte — M. Chopin,
   Andante et Impromptu   Chopin
   No 8   36
2. Romanza — Mme Giulietta Adelasio de Marguerittes
   La Camelia   Guglielmo
3. Piano-forte — M. Chopin
   Etudes, No 25   Chopin
4. *Melodie et Romance* — Mme Adelasio,
   Le Lac — Meditation poetique de Lamartine
   mise en Musique — par   Niedermeyer

5. Piano-forte — M. Chopin,
   Nocturnes et Berceuse, Nos. 27, 59, & 61 Chopin
   Op. 27 & 55   Op. 57

6. *Barcaruola* — Mme Adelasio,
   La notte è bella   Guglielmo

7. Piano-forte — M. Chopin,
   Prelude, Ballade, Mazourkas, Valses   Chopin
   Op. 28   Op. 38   Op. 7   Op. 64

To commence at half-past two o'clock

Tickets, Limited in Number, Half-a-Guinea Each,
and full particulars, to be had of Mr. Muir Wood,
42 Buchanan Street

Sir James Hedderwick, a Glaswegian commentator and diarist, also attended the concert. An ardent music lover, Sir James frequently travelled abroad to listen to the great pianists on the European circuit, so it was an agreeable change when a pianist of international repute chanced upon his own doorstep. He confided his impressions in his diary that night:

> It was obvious indeed, that a number of the audience were personal friends of M. Chopin. No portrait of that gentlemen had I seen; no description of him had I ever read or heard; but my attention was soon attracted to a little fragile looking man, in pale grey suit, including frock-coat of identical tint and texture, moving about among the company, and occasionally consulting his watch, which seemed to be in shape no bigger than an agate stone, on the forefinger of an alderman. In this small grey individual I did

not hesitate to recognise the musical genius we had all come to see. Whiskerless, beardless, fair of hair, and pale and thin of face, his appearance was interesting and conspicuous; and when, after a final glance at his miniature horologe he ascended the platform and placed himself at the instrument of which he was so renowned a master, he at once commanded our attention.

I had frequently seen Thalberg sitting with serene countenance banging out some air with clear articulation and power, in the midst of perpetual coruscations of the most magnificent 'fioriture'. Liszt too, I had often beheld tossing his fair hair excitedly, and tearing the wild soul of music from the ecstatic keys — but the manner of Chopin was different. No man has composed piano music of more technical difficulty. Yet with what consummate sweetness and ease did he unravel the wonderful varieties and complexities of sound! It was a drawing room entertainment, more piano than forte, though not without occasional episodes of both strength and grandeur. He took the audience, as it were, into his confidence, and whispered to them of zephyrs and moonlight rather than of cataracts and thunder. Of the whirl of liquid notes he wove garlands of pearls. The movements and combinations were calculated to excite and bewilder. They were strange, fantastic, wandering, incomprehensible, but less fitted, on the whole, for the popular concert hall than for the salon of a private mansion.

Chopin was always nervous before a performance, and hated delays. Since it was customary for VIPs to arrive late at functions, the knock-on effect of so much aristocracy trying to arrive late meant that the concert

in fact started at 3 p.m. instead of at 2.30. Sir James
Hedderwick, in noting Chopin's constant reference to
his watch, was unwittingly describing a very nervous
performer in the throes of stage fright!

After Chopin's death in 1849, Sir James added a
postscript:

> Poor Chopin! the friend, and perhaps the slave
> of the extraordinary Madame Dudevant [George
> Sand], it was clear to me that he was early marked
> for doom. His compositions live and will live! But
> he himself, with all his fine inspirations, was in a
> little while to be laid where neither applause, nor
> criticism, neither glory nor trouble of any kind
> could come.

The *Glasgow Constitutional* thoroughly enjoyed the
event even if its critical faculties were limited to gut
reaction:

> Wednesday afternoon, M. Frederick Chopin, the cel-
> ebrated composer and pianist, gave one of his
> much-lauded Matinée Musicales in the Merchants'
> Hall here. M. Chopin was accompanied by Madame
> Adelasio, a vocalist who has attained considerable
> eminence in her profession. Few professional men
> can boast of such distinguished patronage as has
> been bestowed on M. Chopin here and in England.
> Indeed, Wednesday was the first public concert he
> has given in Britain [*sic*]. The programme con-
> sisted of four selections from the works of this
> highly-favoured composer, performed by himself
> on a Broadwood grand piano, of most exquisite
> tone, and of two selections from Guglielmo, and
> one from Niedermeyer, sung by Madame Adelasio.
> It would be almost superfluous to attempt a length-

ened critique on M. Chopin's performances, but such brilliant effect we have never heard produced by any other performer. His almost infinite diversity of execution takes his audience completely by surprise. With quaint harmonization, and most ingenious contrivance, he passes from grave to gay, swift as a thought. His closing performance noted in the programme as 'Prelude, Ballade, Mazourkas, Valses' seemed an overflowing stream of delicious melody varied beyond description.

The *Glasgow Courier* was more specific:

Yesterday, this distinguished pianist, assisted by Madame Giulietta Adelasio de Marguerittes, gave a matinée musicale, at half-past two o'clock, which was numerously attended by the beauty and fashion, indeed the very elite of our west end. The performance was certainly of the highest order in point of musical attainment and artistic skill and was completely successful in interesting and delighting everyone present for an hour and a half. Visited as we are now by the highest musical talent, by this great player and the other eminent composer, it must be difficult for each successive candidate for our patronage and applause, to produce in sufficient quantity that essential element to success — novelty; but M. Chopin has proved satisfactorily that it is not easy to estimate the capabilities of the instrument he handles, with so much grace and ingenuity, or limit the skill and power whose magic touch makes it pour forth its sublime strains to electrify and delight anew the astonished listener. M. Chopin's treatment of the pianoforte is peculiar to himself, and his style blends in beautiful harmony and perfection the elegant, the picturesque, and the humorous. We cannot at present descend to particular illustrations in proof of these observations, but feel persuaded we only express the feelings of all who attended yesterday when we say that the pianist produces, without extraordinary effort, not only pleasing, but new musical delights. Madame Adelasio has a beautiful voice, which she manages with great ease and occasional brilliancy. She sang several airs with much taste and great acceptance. We may mention that the pieces were all rapturously applauded, and the audience separated with expressions of highest gratification.

The *Glasgow Herald* described the event at some considerable length, even painting a vivid picture of the scene outside the hall, where there was probably chaos in the street as carriages arrived, jostling for parking spaces and favoured positions in the social pecking order:

On Wednesday, M. Chopin, the great French pianist gave a matinée musicale in the Merchants' Hall, under the patronage of the most distinguished ladies of the nobility and gentry of the West of Scotland. At half past two p.m., when the concert was to commence, a large concourse of carriages began to draw up in Hutcheson Street and the streets adjoining. The audience, which was not large, was exceedingly distinguished. Of M. Chopin's performances, and of the style of his compositions, it is not easy to speak so as to be intelligible to unscientific musicians. His style is unique, and his compositions are very frequently unintelligible from the strange and novel harmonies he introduces. In the pieces he gave on

Wednesday, we were particularly struck with the eccentric and original manner in which he chose to adorn the subject. He frequently took for a theme a few notes which were little else than the common notes of the scale. Those who were present at the entertainment would observe this in the *Nocturnes et Berceuse*. This simple theme ran through the whole piece, and he heaped on it the strangest series of harmonies, discords and modulations that can well be imagined. Again, in another subject, one single note of the key was heard with its monotonous pulsations moving through just as peculiar a series of musical embellishments. One thing must have been apparent to everyone of the audience, namely, the melancholy and plaintive sentiment which pervaded his music. Indeed, if we would choose to characterise his pieces in three words, we would call them novel, pathetic and difficult to be understood. M. Chopin is evidently a man of weak constitution, and seems to be labouring under physical debility and ill health. Perhaps his constitutional delicacy may account for the fact that his musical compositions have all that melancholy sentiment which we have spoken of. We incline to the belief that this master's compositions will always have a far greater charm when heard *en famille*, than in the concert-room; at the same time we know that they possess certain technical peculiarities, which must render them sealed treasures to by far the greatest number of amateur piano-forte performers.

This review, which attempted more than the others to describe Chopin's performance in scientific terms, could be seen as an indication of the analytical attitudes that were prevalent in Victorian Britain, even when treating of a romantic concert. A cold analysis, when compared to Sir James Hedderwick's account, which suggested that he just sat back and enjoyed it!

However, the final point about the technical peculiarities of Chopin's music is significant. Virtually the only way to hear piano music was in the drawing-room, or at the very occasional concert. Thus music needed to be accessible to average taste and playable by the average drawing-room performer. Chopin's music is not easy; an average performer will manage some preludes, mazurkas and waltzes, possibly graduating to the nocturnes. This meant that the appeal of the sheet music of Chopin's works was limited.

The choice of programme offers some interesting speculations. Chopin's opener, the *Andante* taken from his *Piano Trio in G minor*, was dedicated to Prince Antoni Radziwiłł — and was possibly included as a compliment to Marcelina Czartoryska, who was born Radziwiłł; while the *Herald's* mention of the 'monotonous pulsations' suggests the all-pervading throb of the G sharp/A flat of the *Prelude in D flat, Op. 28 No. 15*.

As for the *Nocturnes Op. 55*, the dedicatee was Jane Stirling. To include them would definitely have been *de rigueur*.

The *Herald* concluded by damning the hapless Mme Adelasio — whose unenviable task was to be specifically secondary to Chopin — with some very faint praise:

> Madame Adelasio, who sang three pleasing little vocal compositions — one by Niedermeyer and two by Guglielmo — showed much vocal ability. But she evinced a certain lack of enthusiasm, with which we were not at all charmed. This was her first public appearance in Glasgow, probably, and

we believe, she will gain in public estimation the oftener she is heard.

After the concert Chopin returned to Johnstone Castle, taking with him the Czartoryskis who had been invited to dinner, much to Chopin's delight. He was riding high on a crest of euphoria, for he knew that this concert had been a tremendous success. He had played to an audience who not only understood his music, but also loved it. 'You cannot imagine what new life that day brought to me!' he wrote to Grzymała.

Also at the dinner party were Lord and Lady Murray, Lord Torphichen, Muir Wood and Dr and Mrs Lyszczynski, as well as several members of the Stirling clan. It was a splendid occasion when all the resources of Scottish hospitality were brought to the fore, with the glittering table laden with bone china, crystal and silverware. The company feasted on game, salmon and venison, with varied sweet delights to follow. For once Chopin was happy to stay at the table talking the night away as the port was passed round, although he probably opted for drinking in adulation rather than alcohol. It was at times like this that he felt that Scotland was so like his own native Poland in so many ways, and that night he went to bed a happy man.

CHAPTER SEVEN

Keir House

Keir House stands on a forested slope beside the motorway exit for Dunblane. It commands a spectacular view
of the wide, flat valley between Dunblane and Stirling,
and on a clear day the jagged contours of Stirling Castle
atop its hill are clearly visible. A mile away flows the
Allan Water, which has been so aptly celebrated by
Robert Burns:

> I listen'd to a lover's sang
> An thought on youthfu' pleasures monie
> And aye the wildwood echoes rang;
> 'O, my love Annie's very bonny.'

Antoninus' Wall, the ancient Roman fortification dat-
ing back to *circa* AD 140, ran north from Stirling to Keir
and continued on to Dunblane, where Jane Stirling is
reputedly buried in the Cathedral. This pretty region
of Scotland lies in the southern foothills of the Central
Highlands. It is strewn with lochs, burns, pine forests,
castles, cairns and Roman forts.

Lecropt Church stood at the approach to the house,
which was surrounded by a garden renowned for its
flowering shrubs, water garden and yew tree house,
although today the church is cut off from the house
by the motorway. In Chopin's time the nearby town
of Bridge of Allan was a fashionable spa, with saline
springs at Well House.

Chopin wrote that his host at Keir House was 'a
cousin's cousin of our Scottish ladies, and the head
of that clan'. Thirty-year-old William ('Dearest Willie'

49

to Jane and Katherine) Stirling, MA, was a wealthy, cultured bachelor who had inherited Keir House the previous year on the death of his father. He was an avid art collector, and owned many Murillos and other Spanish masters, as Chopin saw fit to mention. He had just published *Annals of the Artists of Spain*, his authoritative treatise on the Spanish School of Art, that April.

Chopin had originally met William Stirling in London at his house at 38 Clarges Street, and the two men had instantly established a warm rapport. Chopin was delighted to accept his invitation to stay in the face of numerous other invitations that he was receiving at this time; for by now everyone was competing for Chopin as a house-guest. Chopin, who suffered influential philistines poorly but politely, described William Stirling as an intelligent and well-travelled man who constantly received members of English society who came north of the Border. He kept what was virtually an open house, and Chopin commented that 'there are usually thirty to dinner'.

William Stirling greatly enjoyed and understood Chopin's music, and even tried to play it himself. In later years Jane wrote of his enthusiasm for the *Ballade in F. Op. 38*, (not in D, as has been misdocumented) and that he had expressed a willingness to study for years in order to be able to play it as Chopin had done at Keir and in London.

In 1865 William Stirling inherited a title on his mother's side, and became Sir William Stirling-Maxwell. Keir House is still there, but no longer in the Stirling family. The Stirling-Maxwell art collection can now be seen in Pollok House Museum, Glasgow, and some of his books are to be found in the Leighton Library in Dunblane.

However, at Keir House the strict Scottish Sabbath reigned supreme, and on Sunday, 1 October Chopin headed his letter to Grzymała: 'Sunday. No post, no railway, no carriage (not even for a ride), no boat, not even a dog to whistle to', thus eloquently conveying his boredom and sense of frustration.

Chopin's condition was deteriorating steadily, and he was becoming increasingly irritable, for one of the symptoms of tuberculosis is being difficult and hard to please, understandable when the sufferer is continually gasping for breath. Yet at the same time rest, quiet and the welcome attentions of his host should have had a soothing effect on his psyche: not so, because when Jane and Katherine tried to divert him by taking him off to visit relations and friends in a desperate effort to relieve his ennui, he didn't like that either.

Chopin's growing depression was not helped by the autumn mists that were now rising from the glens, obscuring the spectacular panorama of Stirling Castle set in a framework of mountains, lakes and splendid parks. He considered this view from his window at Keir House to be 'one of the finest in Scotland'.

It was Chopin who noted, with wry amusement, the current house gossip about Queen Victoria's first train journey from Scotland back to London. Because of high winds at sea, the Queen and Prince Albert had been unable to sail from Scotland to London along the east coast as was their wont; instead the Queen had ignored the 'processions and sailors awaiting her' at the port and taken the night train to London from Aberdeen, having turned up at the station there in a 'most prosaic manner'. She had of course already been using the train to travel from London to Windsor since 1842, but this is the first recorded instance of her travelling by rail all the way from Scotland. The Royal train to Windsor was fitted with a special coach as a matter of course, but one can only speculate on the travelling arrangements that had to be hastily made to accommodate the Queen and her entourage.

Prince Albert must have been delighted to go by train instead of by boat. Like Nelson, he was reputedly a very bad sailor!

Chopin loved Keir House and told Jane that he would like to live there; despite this, his bouts of depression were becoming more and more frequent. He wrote to Grzymała:

> In the mornings I am fit for nothing until two o'clock, and then, when I am dressed, everything irritates me and I continue to gasp until dinner, after which I must remain seated for two hours with the men, watching them talking and listening to them drinking. Bored to death, I let my mind wander in between making polite gestures and comments in French. I make my way to the drawing-room where I must summon up every drop of energy to revive myself a little, as they are then anxious to hear me play — then my kind Daniel carries me up to my bedroom, which, as you know, is on the first floor, undresses me, puts me to bed and leaves me in perfect peace and freedom to gasp and dream until morning, when the whole thing starts all over again.

Although the main reason was worry about his health, he was also viewing the coming winter with increasing alarm and trepidation, for he knew that his performing days were coming to an end. In the meantime, the concert that Muir Wood had arranged for him in Edinburgh for 4 October was now looming large, and he was very anxious that it should be as successful as his Glasgow matinée had been.

Furthermore, he had not managed to compose anything in Scotland, partly because of Jane's tight schedules, whereby he found himself almost constantly on the move, and partly from a lack of inspiration.

'I feel weaker,' he wrote, 'I cannot compose anything, not so much because of lack of will, more because of physical obstacles, as every week I have to struggle my way along to yet another branch.'

One of these branches was Gargunnock House. This was bought at the turn of the century by another of Jane's brothers, Charles, who died there in 1839, leaving behind a widow and an indeterminate number of children. According to apocrypha, during his visit to Gargunnock Chopin wrote a schottische for one of Charles's innumerable daughters. The manuscript does not exist but the music is widely used in traditional Scottish dancing, and is today accepted as being by Chopin.

Gargunnock House, to the west of Stirling, is still in Stirling hands, although since the death in 1989 of the last incumbent, the house is now in trust. When Chopin visited the place it was surrounded by oaks and Spanish chestnuts, with a walled garden, an octagonal dovecote and an ornamental lake. The trees and the dovecote are still to be seen in the extensive grounds, although the lake has been filled in. Inside the house the 1848 Broadwood piano that, according to legend, Chopin played during his visit, is still there.

Another nearby branch to which Chopin was invited to 'hop' was Jane's birthplace, Kippenross House, between Keir House and Dunblane. The House was built by Jane's father in 1781, and it was there that he and his wife Mary had thirteen children, of whom the youngest was Jane herself. One of Jane's brothers was Patrick, who had fought and been injured in the war with Napoleon, and never fully recovered. Since his death in 1816 — the same year as his father — his son John, Jane's nephew, had inhabited Kippenross. Being only a short distance from Keir House, Jane intended to take Chopin to visit her nephew, and had made the arrangements; but on the day Chopin felt particularly ill and declined the invitation.

On that same day Jane brought back for Chopin a rose from Kippenross; but she kept one petal, which she pressed in her Bible. When Chopin's monument was erected in 1850 in the Père Lachise Cemetery in Paris, Jane arranged for a little chamber to be left behind the medallion on the side. Into this little chamber she put a silver cross, Polish coins dated from Chopin's birth and death, and the pressed rose petal from Kippenross.

Kippenross House stands to this day, just off the Dunblane bypass, in its wooden grounds bisected by the Allan Water. It is still in the possession of the Stirling family.

By now, Chopin was suffering considerably from a surfeit of Jane's solicitousness and hospitality, which were becoming more overbearing as the weeks went by. 'No sooner do I get accustomed to one place,' he wrote, 'I have to go somewhere else, because my Scottish ladies give me no peace, and come for me to drag me round all the members of their family. I always give in — they will suffocate me with their goodness, but good manners prevent me from declining.'

Back at Keir House there was a glittering array of socialites, including Lady Belhaven, who was one of the sponsors of Chopin's Glasgow concert. In more optimistic mode, Chopin described the assemblage as 'some very fine-looking, some very amusing, some very strange, some very deaf and even one, Sir Walpool [sic] who is blind. There are dresses, diamonds, pimples on noses, beautiful hair, marvellous outfits, the beauty of the devil himself, and the devil without the beauty!'

On 3 October the entire house party prepared to depart for Edinburgh and the Caledonian Rout, an action-packed week arranged by the local Hunt Committee, consisting of race-meetings, entertainments, dinners and hunt balls. In the midst of all this celebration was Chopin's concert, a prospect that he was looking forward to with mixed feelings.

But he did note with satisfaction that the sun had come out, and he was able to enjoy the spectacular view of Stirling Castle from his window once more, before leaving Keir House for the Scottish capital.

CHAPTER EIGHT

The Edinburgh Concert

Monsieur Chopin Has The Honour
to announce that he will give a

SOIREE MUSICALE

in Edinburgh, on the evening of
Wednesday, the 4th October

Further particulars will be given in future
Advertisements, and may be learned of Mr Wood,
12 Waterloo Place.

It will gratify the admirers of musical talent to
learn that M. Chopin is to give a Concert on
Wednesday evening, next week, when an opportunity will be afforded to artistes and amateurs
of appreciating his extraordinary performance.
Perhaps it is not generally known that M. Chopin
is one of the most eminent composers and
pianists of the day, and during his stay in
Scotland, he has been the honoured guest of
some of our most distinguished nobility, who
have vied with each other in showing respect
to his unrivalled genius. No description can
convey an idea of the exquisite beauty of his
touch, or the effect which he produces on his
audience by the refined musical taste which he
displays. In his hands the piano may be almost
said to become a new instrument, and its tones
softened and mellowed to a degree which no-one

can conceive who has not had the privilege of hearing his performances.

Edinburgh Advertiser Friday 29 September 1848

Although Muir Wood was director of the Glasgow branch of the firm founded by his father, he was still responsible for promoting Chopin in Edinburgh. The shop at 12 Waterloo Place was in the heart of the city, in the extension of Princes Street.

Muir Wood and Jane Stirling had arranged the concert to be held as part of the celebrations of the Caledonian Rout, and with Chopin's friends as well as the Stirling set thronging to Edinburgh during this week, it was bound to be a success.

By 2 October the programme had been decided, much to Muir Wood's great relief, and there was none of the hesitation and alteration that he had endured with the Glasgow concert. *The Scotsman* of Wednesday, 4 October, announced the programme:

1. Andante et Impromptu
2. Etudes
3. Nocturnes et Berceuse
4. Grande Valse Brillante
5. Andande precede d'un Lango [sic]
6. Prelude, Ballade, Mazourkas, Valses

and further stated that the concert was to begin at half-past eight, with the tickets 'limited in number available for 10s.6d. each from Wood & Co., 12, Waterloo Place'.

By 3 October Chopin was comfortably settled in the small second floor nursery at Dr Lyszczynski's. He wrote to Grzymała that although he was to play the next evening he had neither seen the hall nor settled the programme. As the programme in the *Caledonian*

57

Mercury was submitted by Muir Wood, and is exactly the same as the Glasgow concert, it rather looks as though Muir Wood had learned by experience, put in the advertisement without consulting Chopin, and hoped that he would opt for the tried and tested and play the same programme again. After all, if Chopin changed the programme on the night it would not matter, since it was largely his friends that were coming to hear him play.

October 3rd was a fine, warm day and Chopin was even feeling better. His depression had largely left him, and he had met his friend, the Swedish singer, Jenny Lind, on the platform at Edinburgh; she was on her way to sing in Glasgow before going on to Dublin. She had been performing in Edinburgh for the second time, but did not enjoy the same success as in the previous year. Chopin noted this, and put the reason down to lack of novelty, since she had already been heard. This must have confirmed his nagging fear that, however hospitable and kindly his Scottish patrons might be, he could not expect to keep getting rapturous audiences; when his novelty value wore off he also would find his popularity waning.

The Hopetoun Rooms were situated at what is now 70–72 Queen Street. In 1871 the rooms were taken over as a school, and have since been demolished. Today a commercial building, called, coincidentally, Erskine House, stands on the site.

All the tickets were sold to his many friends and admirers who were gathered in Edinburgh at the time, and the hall was packed. The concert was a great success, and Chopin was very pleased with the outcome, especially since he had made money out of it.

The reviews were not merely flattering; they positively eulogised him.

The Scotsman, on 7 October, wrote:

On Wednesday Evening the Hopetoun Rooms were filled with company to hear this celebrated performer. Any pianist who undertakes to play alone to an audience for two hours, must nowadays be a very remarkable one to succeed in sustaining attention and satisfying expectation. M. Chopin succeeded perfectly in both. He played his own music which is that of a genius. His manner of playing it was quite masterly in every respect .... The Donner und Blitzen school of pianists — originating, we believe, in France — has thrown most European young ladies into fits of ecstatic admiration, and into a career of insanely ambitious imitation. The result of such amateur attempts to play this music has been a lamentable failure, and the almost total destruction of good rational pianoforte playing among the rising generation ... M. Chopin's compositions have a peculiar charm, which, however, is only brought out by his own exquisite manner of playing them. We suspect that many of the salient points of melody in his compositions are reminiscences of the popular airs of Poland — of his own ill-fated land, and that the touching expression he gives to these arises from 'feelings too deep for tears'. The infinite delicacy and finish of his playing, combined with great occasional energy never overdone, is very striking when we contemplate the man — a slender and delicate-looking person, with a marked profile, indicating much intellectual energy.

Two hours would not normally tax a healthy, professional performer, but Chopin was forced to summon precious reserves of strength and adrenalin to fulfil his programme.

The comments of the *Edinburgh Advertiser* of 6 October included a review of the audience as well as of the performer:

> This eminent Pianist gave a Soirée Musicale on Wednesday evening in the Hopetoun Rooms, and we have rarely seen such a display of rank and beauty congregated at a similar entertainment. Most of the élite of our Edinburgh Society were present, as well as a considerable sprinkling of strangers. This speaks volumes for the increase of musical taste amongst us. The performances of M. Chopin are of the most refined description; nothing can equal the delicacy of his tone, or rival the lightness of his passages. They fall most deliciously on the ear accustomed to the 'hammer and tongs' work of the modern school. Our limits will not admit of our entering into lengthened description of his system, but we may mention that, while all other pianists strive to equalize the power of the fingers, M. Chopin aims to utilize them; and in accordance with this idea, are his treatment of the scale and the shake, as well as his mode of sliding with one and the same finger, from note to note, and of passing the third over the fourth finger. The gem of this performance, in our opinion, was the Berceuse, although the most popular were the Mazourkas and Valses, with which M. Chopin concluded one of the most delightful musical evenings we have spent.

— Which review was probably written by a friend, or at least an acquaintance.

The *Caledonian Mercury* on 12 October tried to go even further to ingratiate itself with everyone —

even the piano! — by publishing this account from 'a correspondent':

In addition to the numerous matters of interest of which Edinburgh has been the scene during the past week, the fashionable world have been gratified by the performance of M. Chopin, the celebrated composer. This distinguished individual has for some weeks been resident in Scotland, and we trust that he has found, amidst the magnificent scenery of the north, and the hospitality of the nobility and gentry, that repose for the exercise of his genius which the disturbed state of the Continent denies to men of the most peaceful habits and pursuits. We believe that his public appearances in Britain have been limited in number. We may therefore take it as a high compliment to the taste of the inhabitants of the Scottish Metropolis, that he was induced to give a Soirée Musicale at the Hopetoun Rooms, on the evening of Wednesday last. It is by no means our intention to write an elaborate critique on the compositions of M. Chopin, or on his style of playing them. His name affords a sufficient guarantee for their interest and originality. Were we, however, asked to point out the distinguishing features of both, we should say that their great charm consisted in their reality, their utter want of all charlatanism and false pretension. His music is always the result of principle, his performances therefore are certain to be the development of the living genius within. He never attempts to make the piano do that for which it was not intended, but arrests the attention and interests the sympathies of his audience by the purity of his music, and the simplicity and power of his execution. To any person of common discernment it is evident that M. Chopin's talent cannot be confined to any one accomplishment, and of him it may be fairly said that the mind from which such music proceeds is more interesting than even the music itself. We most heartily congratulate the admirers of music in general on the opportunity which has been afforded to them of rendering homage to one so distinguished by his amiable deportment and high genius. The piano M. Chopin played on was one of Broadwood's finest toned instruments.

It would be interesting to speculate as to the identity of the 'correspondent' responsible for this account.

The comments of the Edinburgh *Evening Courant* read as an epitome of Victorian sentimental hype, but are particularly interesting as they suggest that several expatriate Poles were present, and although the Lyszczynskis would have attended, the Czartoryskis had returned to London by this time. This is the only reference to a Polish clique and is not mentioned by Chopin himself at all.

This talented pianist gratified his admirers by a performance on Wednesday evening in the Hopetoun Rooms, when a select and highly fashionable audience assembled to welcome him on this his first appearance in Edinburgh. The first piece was an 'Andante et Impromptu', the opening movement being in three parts, with the theme standing out in alto relievo, as it were, from the maze of harmony with which it was surrounded. This was followed by his 'Etudes', which had more the character of ideas flitting across the mind, than of studies, and were strung together in the most airy and graceful manner imaginable, being executed with that equality of touch and smoothness of style so peculiar to the performer. Among so much musical excellence, it would be difficult to judge, but to our taste, the most delightful performance of the whole was the 'Nocturnes et Berceuse'. The recurrent air in the minor key conveyed to the mind the idea of night with its silence and repose, while the introduced motif fell on the ear as a lullaby, the beautiful simplicity of the melody, with all its sleepy softness, prompting the idea of a cradle song. It was indeed, a charming morceau, exquisite alike in its composition and its performance. The 'Andante et Largo', were also very beautiful, introducing two Polish melodies, somewhat peculiar in style, yet very pleasing. That they went home to the hearts of the performer's compatriots as were present, was evident from the delight with which they hailed each forgotten melody, with all its early associations, as it rung in their ears. The concluding piece was also national, the ballad reminding us somewhat of one of the choruses in Mendelssohn's 'St. Paul' ('How lovely are the Messengers', we think) and, consequently, having less originality than the others, however the mazourkas which followed had that quality to a degree. There was a quaintness about them quite peculiar; the second (being No. 5 of eight mazourkas dedicated to Mons. Johns, New Orleans-Opera 7 [sic] in particular, was full of harmonic eccentricities (we make use of the term for want of a better, rather than to imply a censure), such as required to be heard repeatedly before the ear could accept them; the third part, having for seven bars, G flat as a fundamental bass, forming an accompaniment somewhat like a bagpipe drone, was truly grotesque. Yet there was a character about it which could not be mistaken. In the barbarous strain one might fancy they saw the Volhynian boor at his holiday dance; and, lest the idea be regarded as overstrained, be it remembered that in Beethoven's Pastoral Symphony the village dance is portrayed. The waltz which followed came from the fingers of the performer with a crispness and sparkling brilliancy of style peculiar to himself. Chopin's compositions have been too long before the musical portion of Europe, and have been too highly appreciated, to require any comment, further than they are among the best specimens of classical excellence in pianoforte music. Of his execution we need say nothing farther than that it is the most finished we have ever heard. He has neither the ponderosity nor the digital power of a Mendelssohn, a Thalberg or a Liszt; consequently his execution would appear less effective in a large room; but as a chamber pianist he stands unrivalled. Notwithstanding the amount of musical entertainment already afforded the Edinburgh public this season, the rooms were filled with an audience who, by their judicious and well-timed applause, testified their appreciation of the high talent of M. Chopin.

This concert was recreated on 7 October 1959 at the French Institute in Edinburgh to commemorate the 150th anniversary of Chopin's birth. It was arranged jointly by the Polish Community and the French Institute. The performer was Janet Walcer.

Chopin himself was far more phlegmatic about the affair. He saw little point in concerts, apart from a way of earning money. His pupil, Karol Mikulie, said: 'Chopin played rarely and only reluctantly in public; to exhibit himself was absolutely against his nature.' The truth was that he hated giving concerts, and suffered from terrible stage fright. 'You would not believe what torture the three days before a concert are,' he once wrote to his friend, Tytus Woyciechowski.

Franz Liszt, the consummate showman of the Donner und Blitzen school, was the exact opposite, and revelled in the glory of public performance and the applause that went with it. Chopin once confided to him in Paris: 'I am not fit to give concerts. Crowds intimidate me. I feel poisoned by their breath, paralysed by curious looks and confused by the sight of strange faces.'

Now, he dismissed his impending ordeal by writing to his pupil, Marie de Rozières, in Paris, on the day before the concert: 'But do not imagine that, apart from it being just an engagement, it causes me anything but impatience and exhaustion. But I find here many people who appear to enjoy music; they pester me to play, and I do so out of good manners, but always with new regrets, swearing I will never be caught out again.'

CHAPTER NINE

Wishaw and Hamilton Palace

'If the weather is fine I shall go to the Duchess of Argyll's at Inverary on Lake Line [Loch Fyne], and also to Lady Belhaven's, one of the biggest houses in the country'.

In the event Chopin did not visit the Duchess of Argyll, but Lady Belhaven was at Keir House at the same time as Chopin, and she must have pressed her invitation forcefully, because, on 16 October Chopin wrote to her from Calder asking if he might still take advantage of her invitation, and on which day he might have the honour of presenting his respects at Wishaw.

After the Hopetoun Rooms concert Chopin spent the night with Dr Lyszczynski at Warriston Crescent, but on Thursday, 5 October he returned to Calder, to stay with Lord Torpichen — and Jane.

Jane had now become more than just irritating; she was becoming a serious nuisance. Blinded by her devotion she seems not to have noticed that the frail composer was constantly choking, seemingly coughing his lungs up and spitting blood daily; he had become so weak that Daniel was having to carry him upstairs all the time. She had now evidently overstepped the mark, because Chopin wrote angrily to Grzymała that friendship was all very well, but gave no further claims to anything else.

Nor was Jane the only problem. Katherine Erskine was a staunch and fervent Presbyterian who now took it upon herself to prepare Chopin for the next world.

She would appear in the drawing-room with her Bible and lists of psalms that she felt would set him on the right path. Chopin was a well-lapsed Catholic, with little faith in religion of any kind, and the strict Calvinistic precepts of the Presbyterian persuasion were anathema to him, and he found her ministry utterly exhausting and totally irrelevant. This was to continue until he finally fled to London, and even there she relentlessly pursued his soul, Bible in hand.

Despite the kindness and hospitality of Lord Torpichen, Chopin had had enough, which is why he had written to Lady Belhaven, who promptly made arrangements for his visit. She also had the good sense not to invite Jane. While he was about it, Chopin planned to take up an invitation he had received from the Duke of Hamilton: the travelling might not be good for his body, but he reckoned that a respite from the 'Szkotki' would be good for his nervous system.

When he arrived at Wishaw House, Lady Belhaven's residence near Motherwell, he collapsed and took to his bed to be tended by Daniel. After a few days, he had recovered enough to enjoy a measure of Lady Belhaven's hospitality.

Wishaw House was a turreted, crenellated, asymmetrical castle that stood at the north-west corner of the parish of Cambusnethan, and in the immediate vicinity of the Burgh of Wishaw. The Lords Belhaven lived at Wishaw House from 1810 until it was demolished at the beginning of the twentieth century, probably because it became unstable as a result of extensive coal mining under the estate.

By Thursday, 21 October, Chopin was at Hamilton Palace, staying with the Duke and Duchess of Hamilton. As in most country houses, there was a large house-party, and among the guests were his friends, the Prince and Princess of Parma. Ever since they had been driven out of Italy they had lived in Kingston in Surrey.

This bright young couple shared a sense of humour with Chopin, and he and the Princess used to laugh together over some of the amateur performances they had witnessed, including a long-standing in-joke about a certain English lady at a soirée, whose speciality appeared to be to whistle to her own accompaniment on the guitar. Now they were barely able to control their sniggers when one of the company stood at the piano to accompany herself while she sang a French love song with an execrable English accent. With much sighing and casting of eyes heavenwards, she warbled, 'J'ay ay-may!!'

Chopin and the Princess had low opinions of certain types of Englishwomen, especially the ones who constantly asked for his music under cryptic Victorian misnomers: 'Play your Second Sigh' they would ask, meaning the Nocturne in G major. Or they would say that his playing sounded 'like water', which simile grated on his sensibilities!

'They all gaze at their hands and play wrong notes with great feeling. What a strange lot, God help them.'

Chopin had not enjoyed many opportunities to laugh over the past few months, and the presence of the Prince and Princess of Parma were as a tonic to the otherwise depressed and sick musician; they in turn were delighted to see Chopin again and invited him to stay with them in Kingston on his return to London.

The Duke of Hamilton was a punctilious and courteous host who had been ambassador to the Russian Court in the reign of Catherine the Great. He was a rigid conformist of the old school — as straight as a grenadier in his military coat, tights and Hessian boots. He amazed Chopin, who slyly sketched him in his diary and wrote by the side, 'This one is a duke in boots and spurs, buckskin breeches with a kind of dressing gown over everything.' Chopin never lost the ability to draw sketches and cartoons, with which he used to amuse his fellow pupils at the Warsaw Lyceum.

How mortified the Duke would have been to hear his undress-uniform described as a 'kind of dressing gown'.

However disrespectful this detail may have seemed, it showed that Chopin's sense of humour was still intact, which was just as well, because the long evenings at table were now impossible for him to bear, particularly as he was in pain when he tried to sit still for any long period. He pointed out that although he breakfasted in his own room, came down late and was carried up and down the stairs, it was still too much for him.

His laughter was still counterbalanced by bouts of depression, and in a fit of misery and despair he wrote out his will, and ornamented it with little drawings of graves and crosses.

The Duke tried to invite Chopin to return to Hamilton Palace when the weather improved, and to take a trip to the Isle of Arran, which he owned. Although Chopin made accepting noises, he knew in his heart of hearts that he would never return.

The Duke of Hamilton died in 1852, and was buried in the Mausoleum he had already built in the grounds to receive his bones. At the beginning of the twentieth century the coal-mines that ran under the Estate collapsed, and the Palace suffered serious subsidence, and became a dangerous ruin. It was finally demolished in 1922, and the grounds bought by the town council. The area, bisected by the M74 motorway between Hamilton and Motherwell, is now the Strathclyde Country Park. The only relic of the Hamilton estate is the Mausoleum, which is preserved in the grounds, and a Roman fort.

Chopin arrived back in Edinburgh on 25 October, sick with fever from the cold that he had endured during the 60-mile return journey; the laughter shared with the Princess of Parma was a distant echo in the dark recesses of his soul.

CHAPTER TEN

Farewell to Scotland

Chopin returned to the tender care of Dr Lyszczynski, ill with a feverish cold, sick at heart and short of breath. A favourite Scottish tonic at the time for being chilled to the marrow was a good dose of red wine, nutmeg and ginger — a popular and efficacious alternative to hot toddy. Mrs Lyszczynski may well have called on its beneficial effects for her guest. However, it was no cure for the greater ills. Chopin's health was now declining at an alarming rate, with his tuberculosis gaining ground daily, and his reserves of strength almost gone.

The University of Edinburgh was founded in 1583. Medical faculties in universities were rare, but in the middle of the nineteenth century the Faculty of Medicine in Edinburgh, like the one in Glasgow, was a far-sighted and enlightened centre of medical teaching and discovery, despite the blot on its reputation for excellence created by the questionable activities, twenty years before Chopin's visit, of the infamous Burke and Hare. Among its distinguished men of medicine was the eminent anatomist, Sir Charles Bell, who held the Chair of Surgery at the Faculty, until his death in 1842; in 1847, Professor James Young Simpson first worked with anaesthetics; and by 1853 Joseph Lister was already working at the University.

But it was Sir Robert W. Philip who first applied himself in Edinburgh to the study of tuberculosis and established its hereditary and contagious qualities; yet the sad irony is that he did not inaugurate his tuberculosis clinic until forty years after Chopin's visit to the university city.

Tuberculosis, then called consumption, is the result of a bacillus which attacks the lungs, causing them to become inflamed and decayed. The symptoms are fatigue, weight loss, a constant cough and haemorrhage — which causes the coughing up of blood — and pain. Prescribed treatment was rest, a good diet and strict hygiene; today the disease is comparatively rare because of the discovery of streptomycin and PAS. It is now known to be contagious, and the whole family of a victim must be watched.

Both Chopin and his younger sister Emilia contracted the disease in their early teens; there was no doubt that both children became infected at the same time. They were treated according to local lore by having leeches applied to the glands; Chopin himself appeared to recover, although Emilia's condition deteriorated until she died at 14.

But actually Chopin never fully recovered, and remained in poor health for the rest of his life. His consumption returned, and the downward spiral continued, bringing with it the pain, the misery, and ultimately, the knowledge that there was no hope.

Trying to live with this knowledge was no mean feat; he had become a fretful and difficult man, and Mrs Lyszczynski found that he had changed from the charming and immaculately mannered musician of the summer, who had played the piano whilst she sang to friends and neighbours, to a complaining invalid who was never satisfied. His shoes were never black enough, his linen never white enough; he would not get up for breakfast, which he expected to be served in bed; he behaved more vainly than any woman, and could not bear to be contradicted in any way whatsoever.

His irritation increased whenever Jane and Katherine visited the house. For two blessed weeks he had managed to elude them, and had not replied to the daily letters they sent him, perhaps without having even read them. Now they reappeared, presenting themselves on the doorstep of 10 Warriston Crescent wielding handfuls of invitations to visit even more relatives and friends; and, of course, Katherine brought her Bible.

'My kind Scottish ladies, whom I have not seen for a couple of weeks, will be here today,' wrote Chopin to Grzymała. 'They would like me to stay longer fighting my way through Scottish palaces, here, there and everywhere, wherever they want me to. They are kind, but so boring, may God bless them. I get letters every day, but I don't reply to any of them, and whenever I go anywhere, they will come after me if they can.'

The writer and later Lord Rector of Edinburgh University, Thomas Carlyle, was less than complimentary about Jane Stirling, and described her as a 'hoarse voiced, restless, invalid Scottish lady'. It was at this time that Chopin was horrified when he learned of a rumour that was sweeping Paris that he and Jane were about to be married. There was no substantiation to this, except perhaps the impression that Jane was falsely able to sow abroad, and now her machinations were beginning to bear fruit. 'I am closer to a coffin than to a marital bed,' he wrote.

Chopin was a romantic in all senses of the word. His early loves, like those of most young men of sensitivity and imagination, were often tinged by a confusion between reality and fantasy. His first real love as a young man in Warsaw was for Konstancja Gladkowska, who captured his heart when she sang at a soirée at the Conservatoire during his final year in the Polish capital. At first he was content to worship her in secret and from afar, confiding his innermost thoughts to his piano. The slow movement of the F minor Concerto is his most eloquent essay of his feelings towards her.

Chopin's close friend, Tytus Woyciechowski, however, was party to his deepest confidences. He wrote passionately about his ideal, of whom he had dreamed and served faithfully for six months, though without saying a word to her.

It was several months before Chopin finally met Konstancja, when he accompanied her singing; but since he always felt awkward in his romantic exchanges with girls, his relationship with Konstancja never really blossomed, partly because of his basic shyness, and partly because of her casual acceptance of the Russian presence, including dashing young officers, in the city. This was anathema to the fiercely patriotic Chopin, and brought on depressive sulks.

Relief of sorts came in the form of the internationally renowned singer, Henrietta Sontag, who gave a series of performances in Warsaw that same year. Chopin fell in love first with her voice — 'She breathes into the hall a fragrance of the freshest flowers, caressing, stroking, enchanting —', then with the person — 'This messenger from heaven'. Again, his love remained firmly in the realms of fantasy, and never came to anything.

Neither did his crush on his two piano pupils, Princess Elisa ('angel exiled for a while here below') Radziwiłł, who died young, and her sister Princess Wanda ('young, seventeen, pretty and how delightful it was to guide her little fingers').

Chopin left Warsaw for Paris in 1830, where he met and was struck by the dazzling but promiscuous Delphina Potocka, who idolised Chopin the musician, and according to some sources, the man. The affair which reputedly lasted three years was discreet enough to be beyond definite verification.

Despite the original sentiments behind the Adagio from the F minor Concerto, the whole work was eventually dedicated, among other works, to Delphina.

In 1835, Chopin once again fell head over heels in love during a trip to Dresden instigated by Count and Countess Wodziński. Chopin last saw Maria Wodzińska as a little girl in his parents' apartment at the Warsaw Lyceum, where her three elder brothers were boarders. She was now sixteen — talented, mature and very pretty. Chopin was struck as he had never been struck before, and there was even talk of marriage. The affair was overseen by Countess Teresa Wodzińska, Maria's mother, who was very much in favour of the match, although her father, Count Wincenty Wodziński, was kept in the dark, and knew nothing of the affair. The Countess promised the young lovers that she would engineer a favourable response to the match. So it was a starry-eyed Chopin who then returned to Paris, while the Wodzińskis went back to Poland, and for the next few months Chopin and the Countess exchanged correspondence on the subject.

He dedicated his Waltz in A flat Op. 69 No. 1 to Maria.

The following year Chopin and the Wodzińskis met up again in Marienbad, by which time Maria's ardour had cooled. Absence had not, in this case, made the heart grow fonder. Also Count Wodziński had objected to the match — largely because of Chopin's health, which had started to deteriorate. The Countess, aware of the dangers in his frailty, had warned Chopin to look after himself and take life a little more easily while in Paris; Chopin disregarded her advice, and continued to lead the full social life of a Parisian bon viveur, and the consequences were now beginning to show. A musician suffering from consumption was not a good proposition for a beautiful 17-year-old girl with the world at her feet.

The Marienbad visit deflated Chopin and upset him deeply. He tied up all Maria's love letters with a ribbon, and wrote on the front 'Moja bieda' — 'My misery'.

In the midst of this emotional upheaval, Chopin met the woman who was to transform his life completely.

It was during the autumn of 1836, when the composer was 26, that Liszt took him to the Comtesse d'Agoult's salon in the rue Lafitte, one of Paris' most fashionable artistic watering holes. Aurore Dudevant was a 32-year-old divorcee with two children, a spectacular ancestry that included kings and adventurers, a turbulent past, an elegant country estate in the centre of France and a highly successful career as a sensational romantic novelist, which she pursued with a disciplined relentlessness under a pseudonym designed to break down male dominance on the literary scene — George Sand.

She was the complete antithesis to Chopin's youthful romances. Six years older than he was, she was highly attractive rather than beautiful, with fascinating, intelligent eyes that betrayed a more total human being than the pretty girls of his youthful years.

George Sand and Chopin began their affair very gradually. At first, she had reservations about involving herself with a man who was smarting from the breakdown of a 'nearly' engagement, while he needed time to get over Maria, as well as to get used to the idea of an older, more mature woman of the world.

A mutual friend was Wojciech Grzymała, and George Sand enquired of him whether Maria was right for Chopin, or was she likely to deepen his sufferings and melancholy.

Ultimately, George Sand was overwhelmed by both the man and his art, while he found her sensuous and desirable. Their passionate love affair was instigated by George Sand, partly because she was strong-willed and dominant, and partly because Chopin was relatively naïve in matters of love.

The following autumn the couple spent the winter in Majorca with her two children, Maurice and Solange. Maurice's health was poor, as was Chopin's, and it was hoped that a prolonged stay in a mild climate would be beneficial to all. In the event, the trip proved to be a disaster, since the weather was poor, facilities negligible, and the natives suspicious and inhospitable. The Pleyel piano which was ordered had been delayed, and Chopin fell behind with his composition commitments. He returned to France in far worse condition than when he left.

That summer Chopin stayed at George Sand's estate at Nohant, near Châteauroux, where she nursed him back to health, looked after him and gave him the support and encouragement that he needed to express his art.

The next six years were the apex of Chopin's creative career. George Sand made sure that he had everything he needed to compose, and their time was divided between Paris and Nohant, where they spent their summers.

It was during this time that Chopin met Jane Stirling and Katherine Erskine, who were thus in a position to observe his prime. Among his greatest works at this time were the last two Sonatas, the F minor Fantasia, as well as some of his finest polonaises, ballades and scherzi.

The end of the affair came in 1847 as a result of a convoluted series of misunderstandings and circumstances. Two factors played a part. Firstly, there was more than a hint that George Sand was beginning to tire of the relationship, which had become increasingly platonic. She found herself playing more of a maternal role, rather than that of a lover, while Chopin was becoming increasingly dependent on her for support rather than sexual fulfilment.

Secondly, there was the affair of Solange's marriage to the dissolute sculptor, Auguste Clésinger, a match arranged by her mother because of Solange's suspected pregnancy.

Both Maurice and Solange were difficult and rebellious children, the consequences of being brought up in a liberal and undisciplined home climate. Maurice hated Chopin, and was at least partially responsible for the break-up. Chopin and Solange, on the other hand, had always got on well, and because of a lack of communication between all parties, Chopin was seen to support Solange without being party to the full facts behind the hasty marriage. Her mother could not accept this, and, coupled with a suspicion of something deeper between Chopin and her daughter, closed the chapter on their love.

The break-up was observed with increasing interest by Jane Stirling. Chopin was obviously going to need a new George Sand to take him in hand; the new revolution seemed like an ideal opportunity to entice the broken musician out of Paris, to pastures new.

Chopin never contemplated any union with Jane, formal or informal. Even now, he was still smarting from the break-up with George Sand. During her tenure of Chopin's heart, she had loved and managed him, and taken care of him in such a way that he drew strength from her, and produced his finest work.

By contrast, Jane Stirling persistently took all excitement and attention from him, and wore him down without seeming to realise the harm that she was doing; for during her tenure, Chopin produced nothing. She was without a doubt sincere in her feelings, and her kindness and devotion were never in question; but this very kindness and devotion were responsible for her utter blindness to his needs for peace and rest, both physical and mental.

Chopin was in no state to start thinking of marriage to anyone; and even if he were, he made it clear to Grzymała that Jane was far from his thoughts as a wife. He wrote:

> But there must be at least some physical attraction. If I could fall in love with someone who would also love me as I would wish, I would still not marry, because we would have nothing to eat and nowhere to live. Whereas one can struggle along on one's own, for two people it would be the greatest misfortune. I may well expire in a hospital, but I will not leave behind a wife without a crust of bread.

There was an outbreak of cholera in Edinburgh which was only just being contained, and Chopin used this as an excuse to refuse all further invitations. He had no intention of leaving the comforts of Warriston Crescent, where he could benefit from Dr Lyszczynski's medical care and Mrs Lyszczynski's kind and — it must be said — understanding attentions. He had had enough of socialising and being paraded throughout the Lowlands of Scotland, and was now desperate for peace and quiet.

For five days he refused to do anything except huddle over the fire in the little nursery, brooding darkly over his predicament and writing letters, which he now ominously signed 'Yours till Death'. He was deeply despondent about himself and wrote despairingly, 'What has happened to my art? Where have I wasted my heart? I can hardly remember how they used to sing in the old country. The world is passing me by, I forget myself, I have no strength.'

He only emerged and came downstairs to eat dinner, before being taken back to bed again by the faithful Daniel and the ever solicitous doctor.

He thought constantly about his roots, his mother and his sisters still living in Poland, and worried about their future. Poland was in turmoil, and still suffering from her ignominious partition by the Prussians, Russians and Austrians over half a century ago, as well as from a brutal betrayal by the Russians during the past fifteen years. The new dream of nationhood, so nearly realised by Napoleon, and, to an extent, by the Congress of Vienna, was now so much dead wood. Chopin's dual nationality by no means diminished his love for the land of his birth, as is evident by the deeply felt nationalism that pervades so much of his music. His heart always went out to his compatriots, both those in virtual serfdom on Polish soil and in émigré communities in the capitals of Europe, including Edinburgh, Paris and London.

In the wake of the 1846–8 Rebellion, France, Britain and Italy were coping with large numbers of Polish refugees, arriving with tales of oppression and tyranny from their foreign overlords. Lord Dudley Stuart was the president of the Society of the Friends of Poland, with headquarters in Duke Street, St James's, London. He organised a Polish Benefit Concert to be held at the Guildhall, London, on 16 November, and invited Chopin to play. Chopin, enraged and frustrated by the constant bad news from his native land, was determined to do whatever he could for his countrymen, and readily accepted.

On 31 October, Chopin bade farewell to Dr and Mrs Lyszczynski, to Jane Stirling and Katherine Erskine, and all his friends in Edinburgh, and left by train for London.

CHAPTER ELEVEN

Return to London

The train from Edinburgh drew in at Euston that same evening, and it was an exhausted Chopin who was helped onto the platform by Daniel. Carrying him to a cab station he quickly arranged for the composer to be transported to Henry Broadwood's house at 33 Great Pulteney St, Golden Square, where Chopin was to stay while an apartment was found for him by Karol Szulczewski.

On his arrival, Henry Broadwood called in Dr Mallan, a homeopathic doctor used by the Stirling family when they were in London. He used all his expertise in an effort to get the sick man back on his feet again. By 3 November an apartment had been found for him at 4 St James's Place, only a few doors away from Lord Dudley Stuart's home. Chopin was moved there, and remained virtually incommunicado until the performance at the Guildhall two weeks later.

The event was officially — perhaps somewhat whimsically — billed the 'Annual Grand Dress and Fancy Ball and Concert in aid of the Funds of the Literary Association of the Friends of Poland'. In fact this was more of a social occasion than a concert. The highlight of the evening was a grand ball, where the most philanthropic members of London society were able to disport themselves. Princess Marcelina Czartoryska was there, and the following day commented on the dubious level of artistic appreciation among Londoners. The ball was preceded by a short concert, at which Chopin's delicate nuances were largely lost as the audience was more interested in seeing and being seen than in listening to Chopin playing.

An unnamed person present remarked:

> The people, hot from dancing, who went into the room where he [Chopin] played, were but little in the humour to pay attention, and anxious to return to their amusement. He was in the last stage of exhaustion, and the affair resulted in disappointment. His playing at such a place was a well intentioned mistake.

Lindsay Sloper, a former pupil of Chopin's, contributed by conducting a small orchestra in some selections. He also recalled that Chopin played the Etudes in A flat and F minor (Op. 25 Nos. 1 & 2).

However, the occasion was deemed a great success, and Chopin himself, perhaps unaware that he had just performed in public for the very last time in his life, was very pleased with the way he played. Naturally, the many Poles present gave him, as usual, a truly vocal Polish ovation, with the strains of 'Jeszcze Polska nie zginęła' (Poland has not yet perished).

This swirling mazurka was written in 1797 by Prince Michał Ogiński to words by Józef Wybicki. It first came to prominence as a marching song of General Dąbrowski's Polish legions, formed in Italy for the liberation of Poland. It was then known as the Song of the Legions. With the rebirth of the Polish state in 1919, it became the Polish National Anthem. Chopin was particularly close to it, since Ogiński's Polonaises, especially the famous and dramatic Polonaise in A minor, were tremendously popular at the beginning of the 19th century, and were a role model for young Chopin's mastery of the form, which he eventually made his own.

The strains were still ringing in his ears as he

returned to his apartment straight after the concert. He arrived with a violent headache and a couching spasm; because of his desperate need for fresh air he kept the windows wide open, thus letting in the cold, damp and foggy atmosphere of the city.

Apart from the *Illustrated London News,* which mentioned in passing that 'M. Chopin, the celebrated pianiste [sic] was also present and performed some of his beautiful compositions with much applause', the only review of what was to be Chopin's last performance ever, appeared in the *Sun* on 17 November:

> The concert took place in the Council Chamber .... We did not hear the performances under any circumstances of comfort, owing to the pressure that prevailed at the entrances .... M. Chopin played a series of Etudes upon the pianoforte, with all his graceful skill and exquisite refinement of style. We should, however, have listened to him with more satisfaction in the retirement of the drawing room than amid such a disturbed and unreflecting multitude as this. The qualities which give him his special charm are too delicate and intellectual to challenge the favour of a crowd bent chiefly on physical enjoyment.

In the meantime, the *Szkotki* had followed him down from Scotland. Katherine called regularly to discuss the after-life with him, armed with her Bible, and to assure him that the next world would be better than this one; to help him pass the time she marked up psalms for him to read, while Jane, with the best intentions, succeeded only in irritating him further.

> One day longer here and I shall go mad, not die. My Scottish ladies are so boring, may God's hand

protect me. They have attached themselves so tightly that it is impossible to shake them off.

Chopin specially wrote of close friends who visited him regularly and were particularly supportive at a time when he needed support most.

Princess Marcelina was living with her husband and young son in Chopin's old apartment in Dover Street; the young couple visited him every day and did their best to console him. Marcelina especially was like a breath of fresh air to the ailing composer.

Henry Broadwood also came regularly, as did that stalwart member of the Polish community, Karol Szulczewski. Born in 1814, he was five years Chopin's junior. As a 17-year-old rebel he had taken to the streets of Warsaw during the initially successful uprising of November 1830, and had joined General Bem's artillery units against the Russian forces. The following year he fought bravely but futilely at the disastrous Battle of Ostrolęka, north east of Warsaw, which led to the defeat of the Poles by the Russians. He was decorated by General Bem, under whom he continued to serve in the Hungarian campaign against the Austrians; he also ferociously defended the barricades of Vienna when that city erupted in riots and unrest.

After the failure of the Polish risings, he eventually came to London by way of Paris. Now in his thirties, his revolutionary tendencies were channelled to desk rather than battlefield, and in 1845 he became Secretary to Lord Dudley Stuart's Association of the Friends of Poland. He and Chopin first met in London during the summer of 1848, and they had struck up a particularly close — if ultimately very short — friendship.

By now Chopin was being attended by both Dr Mallan and the personal physician to Queen Victoria, Sir James Clark. They both realised that he had reached the terminal stage of his illness, and deemed that it would be best for him to be at his own home at the end. They both gave the same advice – to leave London and its polluted air at once and return to Paris.

'Tomorrow I go back to Paris, hardly able to crawl, and weaker than ever,' Chopin wrote to George Sand's daughter, Solange, on 22 November after his doctors had ordered him to leave London. His face was swollen with neuralgia, and he could neither breathe nor sleep. Apart from the concert at the Guildhall, he had not left his bedroom since 1 November. 'I just cannot breathe here, the climate is terrible for anyone in my condition.'

A daguerreotype — an early type of photographic process — taken of Chopin on his return to Paris, shows his face screwed up with pain, his arms folded protectively across his chest, his hands clenched and his face swollen almost out of recognition. His weight had gone down to six and a half stones.

His letter to Grzymała is almost a cry of agony: 'Why does God not kill me off straightaway, instead of little by little?'

On 23 November Chopin left London, accompanied by Daniel and another Pole, one Leonard Niedźwiedzki. Once again, Henry Broadwood bought three tickets — one for Chopin, one for his feet and one for Daniel.

CHAPTER TWELVE

The Final Chapter

Frederick Chopin died at 12 Place Vendôme, Paris, in the early hours of the morning on 17 October 1849, surrounded by friends and family.

At his bedside were his sister Ludwika who had come from Poland, Princess Marcelina Czartoryska, Auguste Franchomme and Jane Stirling. And, of course, the faithful Daniel.

The whole of Paris stopped on the day of his funeral at the Madeleine. His own *Marche Funebre,* the slow movement from his Sonata in B flat minor, was played as his body was brought into the black draped church, and the orchestra and chorus of the Conservatoire sang Mozart's *Requiem,* which he had requested.

Then his body was taken to the Père Lachaise cemetery, with Prince Adam Czartoryski, father-in-law of Princess Marcelina and Giacomo Meyerbeer heading the procession. The pall bearers were his friends Auguste Franchomme, Eugène Delacroix who had painted his portrait, Camille Pleyel and Prince Aleksander Czartoryski.

After a simple prayer his body was buried, but his heart was taken back to Poland and placed in the wall of the Church of the Holy Cross in Warsaw.

Jane Stirling wore black for the rest of her life — like a widow. Before her death on 6 February 1859 she worked tirelessly to collect, buy and send to Poland all of Chopin's works, effects and furniture, including his piano, to form the nucleus of a collection for a Chopin Museum.

It was to be her last mistake. In 1863 a gang of Russian Cossacks plundered the palace where they were preserved, and deliberately selecting all the items from the Chopin museum, including his piano and the original Ary Scheffer portrait of Chopin, piled them up and made a bonfire of them, in a barbaric attempt to destroy Poland's musical heritage.

But as the music critic Carl Engel wrote in Manchester in 1848: 'Although a state of feeble and sinking health leaves little hope for more of these fresh and powerful works, yet it may be safely predicted that by those he has already given us, his name will live — when many of his now more lauded and better-known competitors for fame are forgotten.'

Bibliography

Atwood, William G., *The Lioness and the Little One.* Columbia UP, New York 1980.

Bone, Audrey Evelyn, *Jane Wilhelmina Stirling.* Private publication, Chipstead 1960.

Berlioz, Hector, *Memoirs.* Trans. David Cairns. Gollancz, London 1974.

Brookshaw, Susanna, *Chopin in Manchester.* Private publication, Unknown, 1938.

Chopin, Frederick, ed. Arthur Hedley, *Selected Correspondence.* Heinemann, London 1957.

Chopin, Frederick, ed. Dr H. Opieński, *Letters.* Dover Publications, New York 1988.

Delaigue-Moins, Sylvie, *Chopin chez George Sand à Nohant.* Les Amis de Nohant, Chateauroux 1986.

Eigeldinger, Jean-Jacques, *Chopin Pianist & Teacher.* Cambridge, University Press 1986.

Ganche, Edouard, *Frédéric Chopin: Sa Vie et ses Oeuvres.* Mercure de France, Paris 1921.

Ganche, Edouard, *Dans le Souvenir de Frédéric Chopin.* Mercure de France, Paris 1925.

Ganche, Edouard, *Voyage avec Frédéric Chopin.* Mercure de France, Paris 1934.

Hadden, J. C., *Chopin.* Unknown, London 1903.

Halle, Sir Charles, *Life and Letters.* Smith, Elder & Co, London 1896.

Harasowski, *Skein of Legends Around Frederick Chopin.* William McClellan, Glasgow 1967.

Hedley, Arthur, *Chopin.* Dent, London 1947.

Hipkins, Edith J., *How Chopin Played.* Dent, London 1937.

Karasowski, Moritz, *Life and Letters of Chopin.* William Reeves, London 1879.

Liszt, Franz, trans. J. Broadhouse, *Frederick Chopin.* William Reeves, London 1879.

Maine, Basil, *Chopin.* Duckworth, London 1933.

Murdoch, William, *Chopin: His Life.* John Murray, London 1934.

Naumann, Emil, *History of Music.* Cassell, London *c.* 1900.

Niecks, Frederick, *Chopin as a Man and Musician.* Noevello, Ewer & Co., London 1888.

Paderewski Ignacy Jan, *Memoirs.* Collins, London 1939.

Schonberg, H. C. *The Great Pianists.* Gollancz, London 1964.

Tarnowski, Count Stanislas, *Chopin: As Revealed by Extracts from his Diary,* trans. Janotha, William Reeves, 1906.

Wake, Jehanne, *Princess Louise.* Collins, London 1988.

Wierżyński, Casimir, The Life and Death of Chopin. Cassell, London 1951.

Zamoyski, Adam, *Chopin: A Biography.* Collins, London 1979.

Zamoyski, Adam, *The Polish Way.* John Murray, London 1987.

Periodicals and Newspapers

The Scotsman (1848)

The Caledonian Mercury (1848)

Edinburgh Advertiser (1848)

Manchester Guardian (1848)

Manchester Courier (1848)

Glasgow Courier (1848)

Glasgow Herald (1848)

Glasgow Constitutional (1848)

Edinburgh Evening Courant (1848)

The Times (1840–48)

The Sun (1848)

The Illustrated London News (1848)

Musical Opinion (1848)
Proceedings of the Musical Association, London 1880:
'Reminiscences of Frederick Chopin' by G. A. Osborne.

Index

91